What People Say About Our Excel

I0009501

I learnt that Excel has many more functions that I'm not aware of. It opens my mind in exploring more and thinking of how I can make use of it to collect data. I'm hoping the knowledge gained here will help me do data query and improve my productivity. I want to cut down the time needed to collate data and present it in good visual presentation too. I think I should be able to do that now.

Ivy Low, Administrative Executive, Breastfeeding Mothers' Support Group

I now have a much better understanding of what can be done using Excel for my business and also know how to do it! As the course has real examples and each case study is a build up, it is easy to understand the context and immediately make reference to my own company and problems I have faced.

Neeraj Sundarajoo, Senior Consultant , Comwerks Interactive

I discover the power of pivot tables and charts which allows me to chart very quickly. I now know what my staff can do to extract data and better design forms for feedback survey after each talk or event.

Ho Sun Yee, CEO, Singapore Heart Foundation

Macros and all the functions taught will shorten a lot of processing time for analysing data. Organisation and management of data becomes easier and more efficient.

Anson Yoo, Business Manager, HighPoint Community Services Association

First Published June 2008

Published by:
everydayExcel Business Lab Pte Ltd
15 West Coast Highway #02-07
Pasir Panjang Building
Singapore 117861
Tel : 6873 9946
Fax: 6795 7250

www.everydayexcel.com
Email: jason.khoo@synergyworks.com.sg

ISBN 978-981-08-0914-0

Cover design by Rank Books

Copyright © Jason Khoo

All Rights Reserved. No part of this publication may be reproduced or copied in any form or by any means - graphic, electronic or mechanical, including photocopying, recording, taping or information retrieval systems - without written permission from the author.

Conditions of Sale: This book is sold subject to the condition that it shall not, by way of trade or otherwise, be lent, resold, hired out or otherwise circulated without the publisher's prior consent in any form of binding or cover other than that in which it is published and without a similar condition including this condition being imposed on the subsequent purchaser.

While every reasonable care is taken to ensure the accuracy of information printed, no responsibility can be accepted for any loss or inconvenience caused by any error or omission.

Preface

How to Use Microsoft® Excel Differently from Most Marketers to Gain a Productive Edge

This book is a compilation of a total of 18 practical business case studies used in EverydayExcel Business Lab's Microsoft® Excel course, **"Sales Performance Analytics with Excel"**. The course was created as a result of my friends' and colleagues' repeated requests to recommend an Excel course that could show them how to work on their organisations' sales performance data for analysis in Excel in the same efficient way as I was able to. As I was not able to find one that fit my idea of how Excel should be used for analysis, I eventually decided to put together a course myself. Since then, hundreds of people have attended this course and benefited from it.

There are two parts to this book:

Part One consists of business case studies intended to introduce key concepts for the effective management of data, analysis of information, and reporting of findings using Microsoft Excel. The case studies will walk you through the entire process of manipulating raw data to reporting and showing you how to use Excel in the various stages of data management. It also illustrates how you can harness the power of formulas beyond their basic purpose. The intention is to lay the foundation for you to explore Excel on your own after you have completed the book. It will also make you less reliant on your IT staff and help you achieve an instantaneous turnaround, which you never thought was possible.

In-between case studies, we will also share with you some useful tips and tricks for navigating, selecting, and formatting data lists.

Part Two contains cases studies collected and developed over the years as we helped users address and solve real problems they encountered. It involves advanced formulas and in-depth application of Excel. Without Part I, some users may not be able to follow the concepts discussed in this section. The titles and subtitles are deliberately written in a language that can be easily understood by business users unfamiliar with the lingo used in regular computer books. From the table of contents, you can easily and quickly find solutions to your problem even if you are not familiar with the formulas or functions beforehand. After working through the case studies in this book, you will discover there are multiple ways to use a formula, depending on how you apply it, and you will be surprised that Excel templates can be made very intelligent and dynamic for varied analysis scenarios.

About The Author

Jason Khoo is the founder and chief trainer of everydayExcel Business Lab Pte Ltd, a company which has successfully differentiated itself by offering Microsoft® Excel Courses that empower participants with knowledge of applying the different functions and formulas in Excel to real business needs and scenarios.

An expert in spreadsheets and databases, Jason also founded SynergyWorks, a consultancy firm which has helped many companies extract valuable information from databases using Microsoft® Excel. He has helped companies save significant amount of money by providing solutions using existing PC applications such as MS Excel instead of purchasing new systems.

His clients include multi-nationals corporations such as Discovery Asia, 3M, NCS, Cold Storage, etc.

Prior to setting up SynergyWorks and everydayExcel Business Lab Pte Ltd, Jason has worked in local listed companies and foreign MNCs supporting the marketers in their analysis of marketing plans and providing quality information for business strategic planning and decision-making. He was also a financial counsel for a business unit in a Fortune 500 company which generates a total revenue of more than S$100 million per annum.

Table of Contents

PART I

(Case Studies Download: http:\\www.everydayexcel.com\book)

Tips and Tricks 1

Use [End] **key and** [←] [→] [↑] [↓] **keys to move around large data list.**

1.   Put your cursor within the data list.

2.   Press [End] key once such that the word **END** will appear at the bottom right corner of the worksheet.

   i.   Press [↓] key to move to the bottom of the list or the first blank cell down the list.

   ii.   Press [↑] key to move up to the first row of the data if you are in the middle of the data list.

   iii.   Press [←] key to move to the furthest left of data list.

   iv.   OR, press [→] key to move to the furthest right of the data list.

Case 1: How to find month from dates

Key Learning Points: (*f*x) *MONTH* formula, (*f*x) *COUNTIF* formula, (*f*x) *SUBTOTAL* formula,

F4 key during Edit Mode.

Case Study:

You have maintained a listing of your customers and their birthdays for sending birthday cards before their birthdays. However, it is easy to miss out one or two customers each month because it is very difficult to read the dates and the normal sort function is not able to sort the birthdates by birthday month.

	A	B	C
1	Name	Date of Birth	
2	Adella	18/12/1955	
3	Allen	26/8/1963	
4	Anne	29/10/1947	
5	Beverly	2/1/1971	
6	Bonnie	28/12/1961	
7	Brian	16/10/1979	
8	Carol	2/4/1971	
9	Christopher	9/11/1966	
10	Coral	11/11/1961	
11	Daryl	28/8/1937	
12	David	18/5/1962	
13	David	28/10/1956	
14	David	2/8/1962	
15	Deborah	2/7/1956	
16	Dolores	6/3/1970	
17	Donna	10/2/1962	
18	Donna	21/3/1972	
19	Edward	9/4/1963	

You hope to improve the list by adding another column which shows the birthday month of your customers and also able to filter the list such that you would never miss another customer's birthday again.

Working Files:

1. 1.How to find month from dates.xls
2. 1.How to find month from dates-soln.xls

If we sort the birthdays by ascending order, the records will be re-arranged from the oldest birthday to the youngest birthday. Excel will not re-arrange and group them by month as what most of you have expected. This is because:

Excel stores Dates as Numbers

Excel stores dates as numbers (specifically integers) or sequential serial number in the worksheet. Starting from 1 Jan 1900 as value 1, the date 1 Jan 2006 has a numerical value of 38718 as 1 Jan 2006 is 38718 days away from 1 Jan 1900. However, the interpretation is true only for dates on and after 1 Mar 1900. Go to (http://support.microsoft.com/default.aspx?scid=kb;en-us;214058) for more information.

Excel stores Times as Decimals

What about time? Excel stores time as decimals. 1 day is equal to 24 hours. Therefore, 12 hours is equal to 0.5 (12 hours divided by 24 hours) or 0.5 day. On the same basis, 3 hours is equivalent to 0.125, computed by taking 3 divided by 24. Therefore, if you are to enter the number 38718.125 into a cell and format the cell to show the date time format, it will show 1 Jan 2006, 3 am.

Solution:

1.1 Retrieve part of the date (day, month or year) using *(fx)* Date & Time formulas.

   a.   Enter the *(fx) MONTH* formula **=MONTH(B2)** in cell C2. Cell B2 holds the birth date of your first customer.

	A	B	C
1	Name	Date of Birth	
2	Adella	18/12/1955	=month(B2)
3	Allen	26/8/1963	
4	Anne	29/10/1947	
5	Beverly	2/1/1971	
6	Bonnie	28/12/1961	
7	Brian	16/10/1979	
8	Carol	2/4/1971	
9	Christopher	9/11/1966	
10	Coral	11/11/1961	
11	Daryl	28/8/1937	
12	David	18/5/1962	

   b.   Cell C2 returns the answer **12** which is the month of December.

1.2 Two methods to fill up the formula quickly down a list.

Method 1

a. Copy the formula in cell C2.

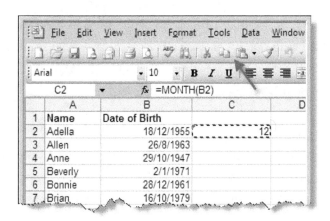

b. Select cell B2. (Step 1 as shown in the picture below)

c. Press [End] key once and let go, the word **END** will appear at the bottom right corner of the worksheet (Step 2 as shown in the picture below); press [I] key. It will bring you down to the last record in Column B. Move the active cell to the right. In this case, it is cell C76.

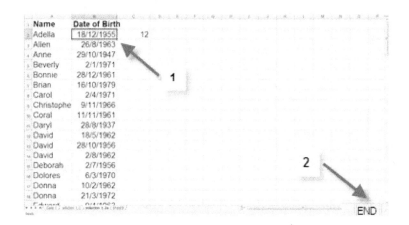

d. Press ⌗ [End] key once; press and hold [Shift] key; press [↑] key. This will highlight the entire range from cell C76 to cell C2.

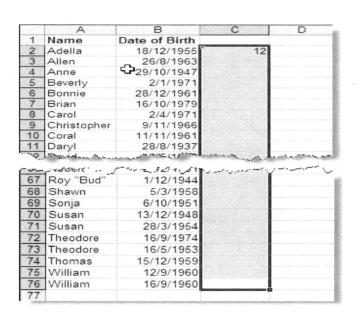

	A	B	C	D
1	Name	Date of Birth		
2	Adella	18/12/1955	12	
3	Allen	26/8/1963		
4	Anne	29/10/1947		
5	Beverly	2/1/1971		
6	Bonnie	28/12/1961		
7	Brian	16/10/1979		
8	Carol	2/4/1971		
9	Christopher	9/11/1966		
10	Coral	11/11/1961		
11	Daryl	28/8/1937		
67	Roy "Bud"	1/12/1944		
68	Shawn	5/3/1958		
69	Sonja	6/10/1951		
70	Susan	13/12/1948		
71	Susan	28/3/1954		
72	Theodore	16/9/1974		
73	Theodore	16/5/1953		
74	Thomas	15/12/1959		
75	William	12/9/1960		
76	William	16/9/1960		
77				

e. To paste the copied data, click on the 🗐 (paste) icon at the Menu bar. You can also use [Ctrl] key + letter [V] key. The third alternative is to hit [Enter] key.

	A	B	C
1	Name	Date of Birth	
2	Adella	18/12/1955	12
3	Allen	26/8/1963	8
4	Anne	29/10/1947	10
5	Beverly	2/1/1971	1
6	Bonnie	28/12/1961	12
7	Brian	16/10/1979	10
8	Carol	2/4/1971	4
9	Christopher	9/11/1966	11
10	Coral	11/11/1961	11
11	Daryl	28/8/1937	8

5

NOTE: When you do the copying, make sure that the phrase **Select destination and press ENTER or choose Paste** appears at the status bar which is located at the bottom left corner.

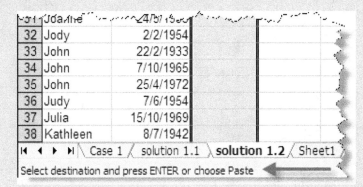

If you do not see it, go to Main Menu, click on **View** and check on **Status Bar** Option in the dropdown list.

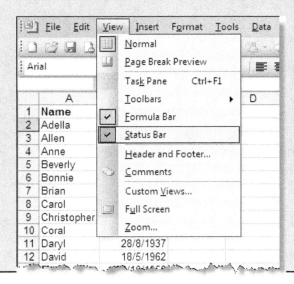

Method 2

a. Move your cursor to the bottom right corner of cell C2 so that a solid **black +** (cross) sign appears.

	A	B	C
1	**Name**	**Date of Birth**	
2	Adella	18/12/1955	12
3	Allen	26/8/1963	
4	Anne	29/10/1947	
5	Beverly	2/1/1971	
	Bonnie	28/12/1961	

b. Double click. Excel will copy the formula down to the last cell making reference to the list on the left, in this case, cell B2 and below until it reaches a blank cell in column B.
Note: Excel will make reference first to Column C. If the cells below the formula (Column C) are blank, it will make reference to the list in column B which is adjacent and to the left of the formula.

	A	B	C
1	Name	Date of Birth	
2	Adella	18/12/1955	12
3	Allen	26/8/1963	8
4	Anne	29/10/1947	10
5	Beverly	2/1/1971	1
6	Bonnie	28/12/1961	12
7	Brian	16/10/1979	10
8	Carol	2/4/1971	4

7

1.3 Count records based on certain conditions

a. To count the number of customers who are having their birthdays in each month, enter the (ƒx) *COUNTIF* formula **=Countif($C$2:$C$76,B81)** into cell C81. **$C$2:$C$76** is the range to search for the results. **B81** is the condition for the count. This means that the formula will count the number of cells in the range $C$2:$C$76 and return the number of cells that are equal to the value contained in cell B81 (in this case, the value is "1"). B81 is used because we want to copy the formula down to the rest of the cells from cell C81 to cell C92. You can use **1** instead but that would mean that the formula is fixed with the count criteria of 1.

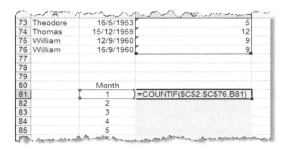

b. Cell C81 returns the value **4**; it means that four persons in the list are born in January. Copy the formula down to cell C92 to get the rest of the answers. The total sum added up for the 12 months should be 75.

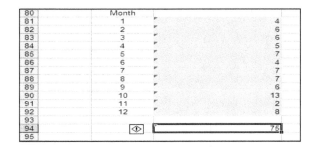

8

The (*f*x) *COUNTIF* formula is used to count the number of cells in a range that satisfies the condition set in the formula. The formula is set up as follows:

= Countif (*Range you wish to perform the count, the condition of the count*)

The condition for the count can be a reference to a cell or a fixed number such as 55. By default, the condition is set as equal to a particular value or cell. But it does not necessary has to be so. You can make the criteria a range such as "<55" e.g. **=countif($C$2:$C$76,"<55")**. This will make the formula count the number of cells in the range where the value contains within each cell in the range is less than 55.

Relative Cell and Absolute Cell Reference and the [F4] key

Take note of the **$** in **$C$2:$C$76**. The purpose of the **$** is to fix the range such the range will not move as we copy the formula down to the other months (**Absolute Cell Reference**). On the other hand, **B81** is set as a **Relative Cell Reference** because we want the reference to move as the formula is copied down to B92. The formula will refer to month 2, 3 and so on as it is copied down column B. You can actually rotate the cell referencing by pressing [F4] key as you continue to type in the formula.

9

1.4 Filter records based on pre-defined conditions

a. Use the **AutoFilter** Function to identify the name of customers having their birthdays in a particular month.

b. To filter the customers who are having their birthdays in January, first select one of the cells within the list as the active cell. Then activate the **AutoFilter** Function as shown below. (**Data → Filter → AutoFilter**)

Note: For the rest of this book, we will use → to denote navigation from Main Menu to Sub Menu.

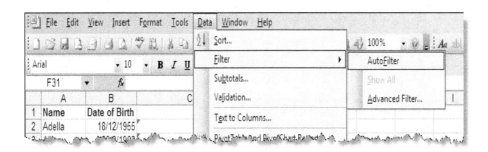

c. Click on the inverted triangle located on the right side of cell C1. Select **1** presented in the dropdown list. With the selection, the list will now show only 4 customers who are having their birthdays in January (denoted by the value 1).

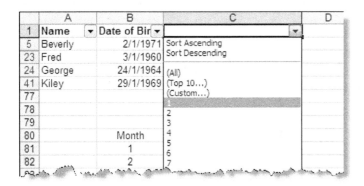

1.5 Count the records of visible cells only

> The (fx) **SUBTOTAL** formula (do not confuse with **SUBTOTAL** function) is like a (fx) **COUNT** formula. What differentiate (fx) **SUBTOTAL** formula from the (fx) **COUNT** formula is in its ability to count the number of the filtered **visible cells** in a range. The (fx) **SUBTOTAL** formula works hand in hand with the **AutoFilter** Function as demonstrated in the example given below.

a. The (fx) **SUBTOTAL** Formula is very useful in counting the number of customers that satisfy the filtered criteria. Go to cell C78.

b. Enter the (fx) **SUBTOTAL** formula **=Subtotal(3,A2:A76)** into the cell C78. The function number **3** in the (fx) **SUBTOTAL** formula indicates that we are interested to count the number of customers who have their birthdays in the month of January. Other numbers indicate different types of calculation. See the list at the end of case 1.4 for more information. **A2:A76** is the range (including the hidden/ filtered cells) that (fx) **SUBTOTAL** formula use to perform the calculation.

	A	B	C	D
1	Name ▾	Date of Bir ▾	▾	
5	Beverly	2/1/1971	1	
23	Fred	3/1/1960	1	
24	George	24/1/1964	1	
41	Kiley	29/1/1969	1	
77				
78		SUBTOTAL	=SUBTOTAL(3,A2:A76)	
79				
80		Month		
81		1		4

c. The formula returns the value **4**. The value changes as you select different months in the dropdown list of the **AutoFilter** Function.

> You need to leave a row between your data records and (fx) **SUBTOTAL** formula. If not, Excel will mistake (fx) **SUBTOTAL** formula as part of the data records for filtering.

d. Replace the function number **3** in (*f*x) **SUBTOTAL** formula to **2** like this =**Subtotal(2,A2:A76)** and hit **Enter**.

	A	B	C	D
1	Name ▼	Date of Bir ▼	▼	
5	Beverly	2/1/1971	1	
23	Fred	3/1/1960	1	
24	George	24/1/1964	1	
41	Kiley	29/1/1969	1	
77				
78		SUBTOTAL	=SUBTOTAL(2,A2:A76)	

e. The formula returns the value **0**. This is because function number **2** in the (*f*x) **SUBTOTAL** formula counts only the number of values in the range whereas function number **3** counts the number of non-blank cells in the range.

f. Change the range in the formula from **A2:A76** to **C2:C76**. The result returns the value **4** because the range C2:C76 contains values, not text.

	A	B	C	D
1	Name ▼	Date of Bir ▼	▼	
5	Beverly	2/1/1971	1	
23	Fred	3/1/1960	1	
24	George	24/1/1964	1	
41	Kiley	29/1/1969	1	
77				
78		SUBTOTAL	=SUBTOTAL(2,C2:C76)	

The purpose of changing the function numbers is to show that the (*f*x) **SUBTOTAL** formula can count text as well values.

g. Now you have a summary showing the number of customers having their birthdays in each month and you also could also find out the names of these customers having their birthdays in a particular month.

	A	B	C
1	Name	Date of Bir	
2	Adella	18/12/1955	12
3	Allen	26/8/1963	8
4	Anne	29/10/1947	10
5	Beverly	2/1/1971	1
6	Bonnie	28/12/1961	12
7	Brian	16/10/1979	10
8	Carol	2/4/1971	4
9	Christopher	9/11/1966	11
10	Coral	11/11/1961	11
74	Thomas	15/12/1959	12
75	William	12/9/1960	9
76	William	16/9/1960	9
77			
78		SUBTOT	75
79			
80		Month	
81		1	4
82		2	6
83		3	6
84		4	5
85		5	7
86		6	4
87		7	7
88		8	7
89		9	6
90		10	13
91		11	2
92		12	8
93			

What other calculations can (fx) SUBTOTAL formula perform other than count?

Function Number	Function	Meaning
1	AVERAGE	Average value for the filtered range
2	COUNT	Count the number of cells that contain values in the filtered range
3	COUNTA	Count the number of non-blanks cells in the filtered range
4	MAX	Returns the max value in the filtered range
5	MIN	Returns the min value in the filtered range
6	PRODUCT	Multiplies the values in the filtered range
7	STDEV	Returns the standard deviation for the sample in the filtered range
8	STDEVP	Returns the standard deviation for the population in the filtered range
9	SUM	Returns the sum of all the values in the filtered range
10	VAR	Returns the variance for the sample in the filtered range
11	VARP	Returns the variance for the population in the filtered range

End of Case 1

Tips and Tricks 2

Pull out the Print Area icon into the Toolbar

1. Pulling out the Print Area icon and put it on the toolbar will cut down additional steps required if the **File → Print Area → Set Print Area / Clear Print Area** is selected. It is especially useful when you regularly need to set different ranges for printing.

2. Right click anywhere within the toolbar area, a popup menu will appear. Click on **Customize** at the bottom of the list.

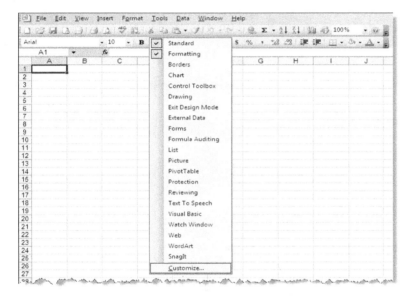

3. A Customize popup box will appear. Select the **Commands** tab. Click on **File** under the **Categories** box, then, at the **Commands** box, scroll down to select **Set Print Area**.

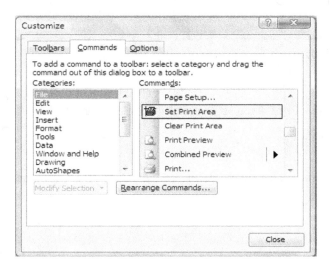

4. Click and hold on to **Set Print Area**, drag and drop it in one of the toolbars on top like this.

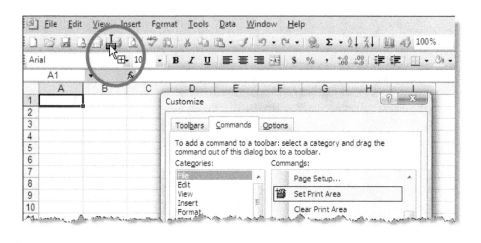

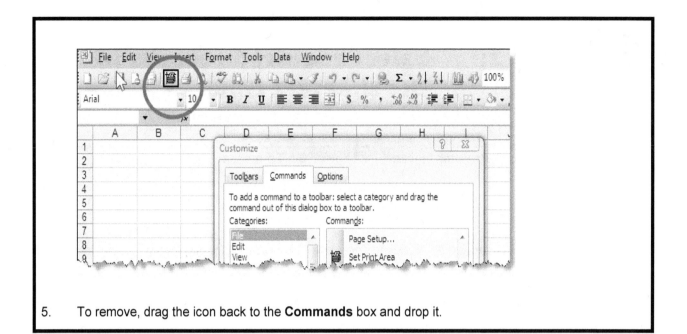

5. To remove, drag the icon back to the **Commands** box and drop it.

Case 2: Select required records in the shortest time

Key Learning Points: **AutoFilter** function, F5 key or **Go To** function.

Case Study:

You have a long list of companies detailing their sales turnover and number of employees each company has. You are told that you need to filter the list and contact those which have a minimum turnover of $100,000 and at least 1000 employees. Subsequently, you need to contact these companies to promote the new product you are carrying.

	A	B	C	D
1	Co Name	Sls Turnover	No Of Employees	
2	01 COMPUTER SYSTEM PTE LTD	33,703	33	
3	3COM ASIA PACIFIC RIM PTE LIMITED	520,122	75	
4	68 SYSTEMS & PROJECT ENGINEERING	11,500	88	
5	A & P CO-ORDINATOR PTE LTD	9,564	69	
6	A.P. MOLLER SINGAPORE PTE. LTD*	386,558	779	
7	AAA INTERNATIONAL PTE LTD	58,931	6	
8	AAF SINGAPORE PTE. LTD.	27,236	108	
9	AAVANTI INDUSTRIES PTE LTD	611,918	9	
10	ABAQUS			
2542		52,975	208	
2543	ZEPHYR SILKSCREEN COMPANY (PRIVA	16,277	150	
2544	ZF SOUTH EAST ASIA PTE LTD	37,907	39	
2545	ZHAN CHANG GRANITE QUARRY PTE LT	15,183	163	
2546	ZHENG KENG ENGINEERING & CONSTRI	27,844	155	
2547	ZHONGJING (SINGAPORE) OIL CO. PTE L	85,978	1	
2548	ZIRCON ENGINEERING PTE LTD	14,277	25	
2549	ZUELLIG PHARMA PTE. LTD.	421,135	294	
2550				
2551				

Because the companies' sales turnover and the employee size are not correlated to each other (companies with high sales turnover does not necessary mean that they have a lot of employees), sorting the list by turnover and then followed by employee size will not work. Excel will return the list sorted by the first criteria only, i.e. by sales turnover. Two criteria sort works only when the companies have the same sales turnover or values. Therefore, a simple sort will not solve your problem.

There are various ways to solve this problem. We will show you one of them. Our objective is to demonstrate the functions that are available in Excel to manage your list and to build your foundation so that you could exploit these functions further on your own.

Working File:

1.   *2.Select required records in the shortest time.xls*
2.   *2.Select required records in the shortest time-soln.xls*

Solution:

2.1   Filter records using a range

a.   Select a cell anywhere within the list, activate the **AutoFilter** Function (**Data → Filter → AutoFilter**)

b.   Click on the inverted triangle in cell B1 (containing the word "Sls Turnover") and select **Custom** from the drop down list.

	A	B	C	D
1	Co_Name ▼	Sls Turnover ▼	No Of Employe(▼	
2	01 COMPUTER SYSTEM PTE LTD	(All)	33	
3	3COM ASIA PACIFIC RIM PTE LIMITED	(Top 10...)	75	
4	68 SYSTEMS & PROJECT ENGINEERING	(Custom...) 6,058	88	
5	A & P CO-ORDINATOR PTE LTD	6,060	69	
6	A.P. MOLLER SINGAPORE PTE. LTD*	6,122	779	
7	AAA INTERNATIONAL PTE LTD	6,180 6,184	6	

c. The **Custom AutoFilter** popup box will appear. Select the sales turnover criteria to be **greater than or equal to** and type in **100,000**; click **OK**.

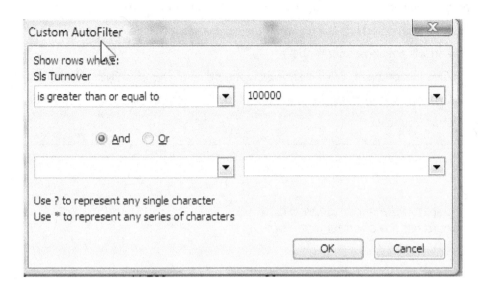

d. Do the same for the "No of Employees" column. Click on the inverted triangle in cell C1 and select **Custom** from the drop down list. The criteria is **greater than or equal to** and the value **1000**.

e. Once filtered, the inverted triangles in cell B1 and C1 as well as the row numbers will turn blue.

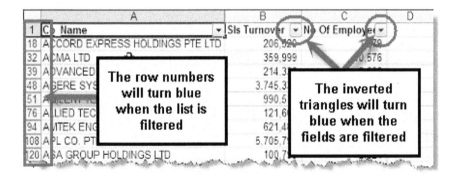

2.2 Select the entire database in 3 simple steps

a. Select a cell within the list. Go to Main Menu and click on **Edit → Go To**. You can also use Ctrl key + letter G key. Alternatively, press the F5 key.

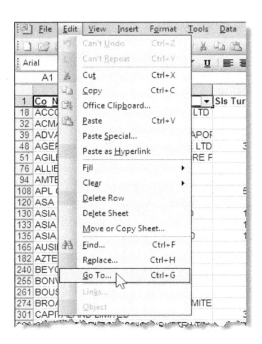

b. In the popup box, click on the **Special** button located at the bottom left corner.

c.   Select the **Current Region** option and click **OK**. This will highlight the entire data range.

2.3   Select only the visible cells within the selected range

a.   Activate the **Go To** function and select the **Special** button again. Select the **Visible Cells only** option and click **OK**.

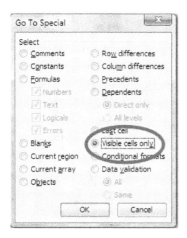

b.   Copy the selected range and paste them into a new worksheet. The list only shows companies which have sales turnover of more than or equal to $100,000 and employee size of 1,000.

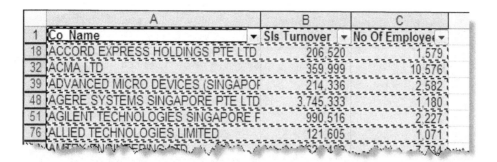

	A	B	C
1	Co Name ▾	Sls Turnover ▾	No Of Employee ▾
18	ACCORD EXPRESS HOLDINGS PTE LTD	206,520	1,579
32	ACMA LTD	359,999	10,576
39	ADVANCED MICRO DEVICES (SINGAPOF	214,336	2,582
48	AGERE SYSTEMS SINGAPORE PTE LTD	3,745,333	1,180
51	AGILENT TECHNOLOGIES SINGAPORE F	990,516	2,227
76	ALLIED TECHNOLOGIES LIMITED	121,605	1,071

If you are using Excel version 2000 and above, the above steps are not necessary as Excel has built in the function such that when you highlight the entire filtered range, it will copy only the visible records. Going through the above step is to show you how Excel does it and to make it easier for you to apply the function in the examples given in the later part of this course.

End of Case 2

Tips and Tricks 3

Presenting the text in 2 lines within a cell

Instead of using **Wrap Text**, typing lots of "spaces" and adjusting the width of the column to make a sentence falls into 2 lines, use ⌨Alt key + ⌨Enter key.

1. Place the cursor in between the words that needs a break. In this case, in the middle of "No. of Employees".

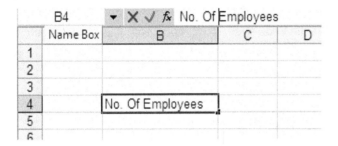

2. Press and hold on the ⌨Alt key and hit the ⌨Enter key once. Let go of the ⌨Alt key and hit the ⌨Enter key again. Note that the two lines remains regardless of any adjustment in the width of column.

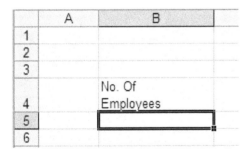

Case 3: More (*f*x) formulas explained

Key Learning Points: (*f*x) *MID* formula, (*f*x) *SEARCH* formula, (*f*x) *ISNUMBER* formula, , (*f*x) *IF* formula, (*f*x) *VLOOKUP* formula, (*f*x) *ISERROR* formula, **Subtotal** function, **Text to Column** function, (*f*x) *SUMIF* formula, (*f*x) *COUNTIF* formula.

Case Study:

As you work on the list (in case 2), you discover that the companies in some industries respond better to the new product better than others. To escalate the calling process, you want to focus first only on those more responsive industries. Then you realised that the list do not contain the industry class. It is in another list as shown. So how could we effectively and efficiently get the company list with its industry class?

	A	B
1	Co_Name	Industry_Class
2	01 COMPUTER SYSTEM PTE LTD	Wholesale - Telecom / Office Apparatus / Computers
3	3COM ASIA PACIFIC RIM PTE LIMITED	Wholesale - Telecom / Office Apparatus / Computers
4	68 SYSTEMS & PROJECT ENGINEERING PTE LTD	Construction - Fittings / Fixtures
5	A & ONE PRECISION ENGINEERING PTE. LTD.	Construction - Structural / Mechanical Engineering
6	A & P CO-ORDINATOR PTE LTD	Services - Printing / Publishing
7	A.P. MOLLER SINGAPORE PTE. LTD*	Comm/Tpt/Storage - Transport - Marine
8	AAA INTERNATIONAL PTE LTD	Wholesale - Electrical / Electronic
9	AAAS COM SOLUTION PTE LTD	Retail - Office Apparatus / Computer / Related Accessories

The name list provided consists of two columns of data. One column contains the company name while the other has the industry class and sub-industry class presented together. For example, cell A2 contains the company named **01 COMPUTER SYSTEM PTE LTD** and cell B2 contains **Wholesale - Telecom / Office Apparatus / Computers**. What you are looking for is just the general industry class **Wholesale**. And what's more, the list does not contain information such as sales turnover and employee size which are information you need to have. How are you going to separate the text and combine the two lists into one?

The primary purpose of this scenario is to show you how formulas can be combined together to achieve the results you want. The secondary objective is to show you that formulas don't work alone. By combining formulas together, you can get the info you want at least 10 times faster.

Working File:

1.   *3a.More Fx formulas explained.xls*
2.   *3a.More Fx formulas explained-Soln.xls*
3.   *3b.More Fx formulas explained.xls*
4.   *3b.More Fx formulas explained-Soln.xls*

Solutions:

Solution 3A

3.1   Retrieve part of the text from a cell

In our example, we key in the formulas directly in the cells. You may find it useful to use the *f*x popup box.

1.   Click on the *f*x icon.

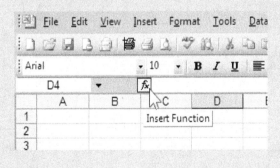

3. The **Insert** Function popup box appears. Type in the name of the formula you want or select a category to find the formulas in the Select a function box.

Insert Function

Search for a function:

Type a brief description of what you want to do and then click Go   Go

Or select a category: Most Recently Used ▾

Most Recently Used
All
Financial
Date & Time
Math & Trig
Statistical
Lookup & Reference
Database
Text
Logical
Information

Select a function:

WEEKDAY
SUM
AVERAGE
IF
HYPERLINK
COUNT
MAX

WEEKDAY(serial_n... Returns a number from 1 to 7 identifying the day of the week of a date.

Help on this function   OK   Cancel

a. We have to remove the sub-industry category from the list located in **IndustryClass** worksheet. Enter the (*f*x) **MID** formula **=Mid(B2,1,9)** into the cell C2. The result returned by (*f*x) **MID** formula is the word **Wholesale** which is the first 9 characters from Cell B2.

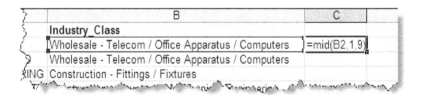

B	C
Industry_Class	
Wholesale - Telecom / Office Apparatus / Computers	=mid(B2,1,9)
Wholesale - Telecom / Office Apparatus / Computers	
Construction - Fittings / Fixtures	

By using the **(fx)** **MID** formula, you can separate the text in one cell into 2 or more different cells.

Here is a sample of the **(fx)** **MID** formula: **=Mid(B2,1,9)**

1. The first part **B2** is the cell which contains the text you want to separate.

2. The second part **1** is the position to start extracting the text. In our case, we start from position 1. If you start from position 2, (let's say we use the word **Wholesale**), the **(fx)** **MID** formula will start extracting from the character "**h**".

3. The last part **9** determines how many characters should be extracted from the cell B2. Using the same word **Wholesale**, putting 3 would extract the 3 characters "**hol**" (starting position is 2) and putting 4 in this part of the formula will extract 4 characters "**hole**".

The **(fx)** **LEFT** formula and **(fx)** **RIGHT** formula work similarly like **(fx)** **MID** formula except that they do not have the second part like the **(fx)** **MID** formula does. As the name of the formula implies, they start counting the position from the left and right of the text referred.

b.   Drag the formula down to row 4. You will find that it doesn't pull out the word **Construction**. Instead, it pulls **Construct**.

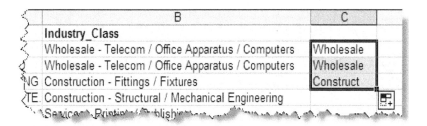

3.2   Retrieve text of varying length intelligently

At row 4, you will notice that the word **Construct** instead of **Construction** appears. This is because the word **Wholesale** has 9 characters but **Construction** has 12. We therefore have to improve on the formula to make sure that the full word is retrieved. The **(ƒx) SEARCH** formula seems so useless on its own but in our example, it can do wonders.

The **(ƒx) SEARCH** formula will return the position where the search alphabet/word is **FIRST** found in the cell. In our example, we find " –"(space and dash) because there is a possibility that there are 2 dashes ("-") within the same cell. By putting in a space before the dash in the search text, we make the search more stringent.

a.   Enter the formula **=Search(" –",B2)** into cell D2. The **(ƒx) SEARCH** formula will return the position of " -" (space and dash). Cell D2 returns the value **10** which is the starting position of the " " (space).

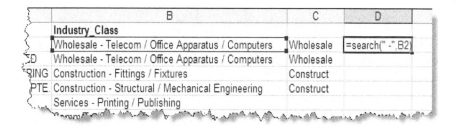

b.   Our word **Wholesale** has only **9** characters but the search result return the number **10**. To get back the value 9, we have to deduct a unit from the result (**10**) returned by the **(ƒx) SEARCH** formula.

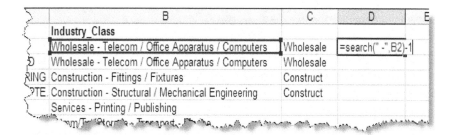

29

If the formula returns a number as in our case of (ƒx) *SEARCH* formula (even though the result meant the 10th position), we can still perform mathematical calculations with the results.

c.   Replace the value **9** found in cell D2 with the (ƒx) *SEARCH* formula **Search(" -",B2)-1**. In the formula bar, highlight the formula without the = (equal) sign. Right click and select **Copy**. *(Note: You can also use* Ctrl *key +* C *key to copy after highlighting the formula).*

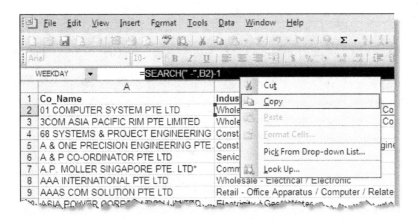

d.   Press Esc key to exit editing mode, i.e. to get out of the formula bar area.

e.   Go to cell C2 and highlight the value 9. Right click and select **Paste**. Hit **Enter**.

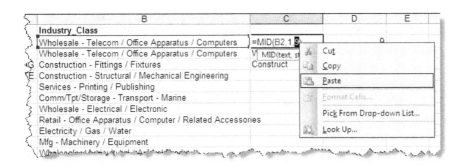

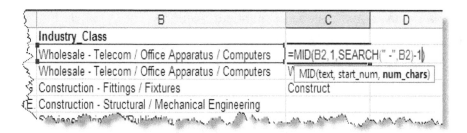

In this step, we are showing you that the numbers contained in each formula can be replace by another formula. Or it can be replaced by a cell reference. This will make your formula more dynamic. This approach will help you unlock the power of Excel which is unknown to many users, even the seasoned users.

f.   Copy the formula down to cell C4. You should see the word **Construction** now appearing in full instead of the partial word **Construct**.

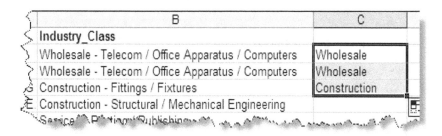

31

g. Copy the formula down to C10. You will find that the cell returns **#VALUE!**; an indication that the formula contains text instead of numbers. A further check shows that the (*fx*) **SEARCH** formula also returns **#VALUE!**. To confirm, copy the formula in cell D2 to cell D10. This error appears because the (*fx*) **SEARCH** formula cannot find any " -" in cell B10.

B	C	D
Industry_Class		
Wholesale - Telecom / Office Apparatus / Computers	Wholesale	9
Wholesale - Telecom / Office Apparatus / Computers	Wholesale	9
Construction - Fittings / Fixtures	Construction	12
Construction - Structural / Mechanical Engineering	Construction	12
Services - Printing / Publishing	Services	8
Comm/Tpt/Storage - Transport - Marine	Comm/Tpt/Storage	16
Wholesale - Electrical / Electronic	Wholesale	9
Retail - Office Apparatus / Computer / Related Accessor	Retail	6
Electricity / Gas / Water	#VALUE!	#VALUE!

h. To address the error, we need to do 2 things:

   i. Identify the error when it appears.

   ii. Do something when the error appears.

For other types of error returned by the Excel formulas, please refer to the list in 3.7.

3.3 Use Error Formula to clean up your data

a. To identify the error, we can use the *(fx)* *ISNUMBER* formula, which will returns **TRUE** or **FALSE** depending on whether it is a number or not.

The *(fx)* *ISNUMBER* formula will return the results **TRUE** or **FALSE** depending on whether a number is found. If a number is found, the formula will return **TRUE**, else it will return **FALSE**.

If you look at the *(fx)* *ISNUMBER* formula, you will once again find that the formula seems useless. But by putting it together with other formulas, you are one step nearer to getting the results you want.

---

b. Type in the formula **=Isnumber(D10)** into cell E10. The formula will return **FALSE**. If you copy the formula from cell F10 to cell F9, the results will show **TRUE** because the cell D9 contains a number.

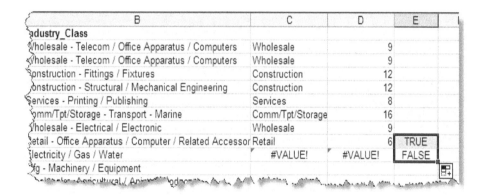

B	C	D	E
dustry_Class			
Wholesale - Telecom / Office Apparatus / Computers	Wholesale	9	
Wholesale - Telecom / Office Apparatus / Computers	Wholesale	9	
onstruction - Fittings / Fixtures	Construction	12	
onstruction - Structural / Mechanical Engineering	Construction	12	
ervices - Printing / Publishing	Services	8	
omm/Tpt/Storage - Transport - Marine	Comm/Tpt/Storage	16	
holesale - Electrical / Electronic	Wholesale	9	
etail - Office Apparatus / Computer / Related Accessor	Retail	6	TRUE
lectricity / Gas / Water	#VALUE!	#VALUE!	FALSE
fg - Machinery / Equipment			

We would need to give Excel some instruction to work on the 2 outcomes, **TRUE** and **FALSE**, from the (*f*x) **ISNUMBER** formula.

The first result, **TRUE**, indicate that the (*f*x) *SEARCH* formula will return a number, i.e. it is able to find a " –
" in the industry description for the company.

The second result, **FALSE**, indicate that " –" cannot be found.

The (*f*x) *IF* formula will be able to address the above 2 outcomes.

c.   Enter the (*f*x) *IF* formula **=If(E10=TRUE,C10,B10)** in cell F10. The (*f*x) *IF* formula will check the (*f*x) *ISNUMBER* formula in cell E10. If the result is **TRUE**, it returns the value in C10 which shows the general industry class description. If it is **FALSE**, then it returns the value in B10. In cell F10, it returns the industry class **Electricity / Gas / Water**.

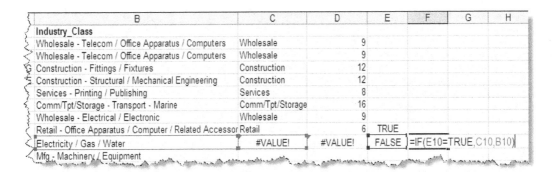

d.   To reduce the number of columns, we could replace the cell references in cell F10 with the formulas in cell E10 and cell C10 respectively. For example, we could replace the cell reference E10 in the formula **=If(E10=TRUE,C10,B10)** with the formula in cell E10 which is **=ISNUMBER(D10)**. After replacing the cell reference E10, you should have **=If(ISNUMBER(D10)=TRUE,C10,B10)**.

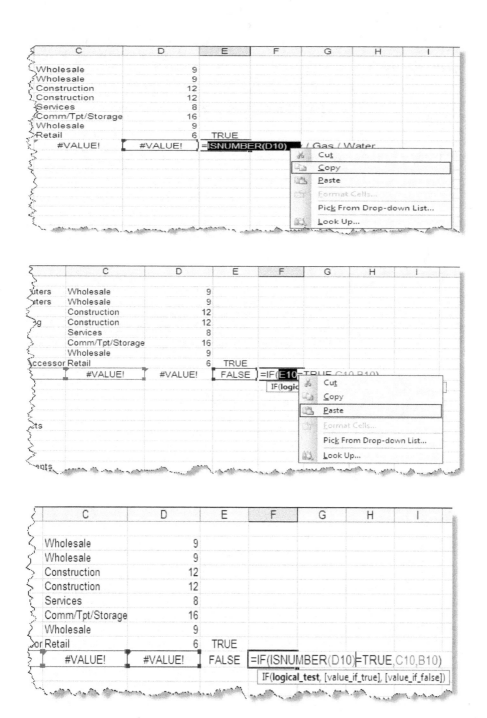

e. Repeat the process for D10 and C10 in the formula. After you have completed replacing all the formulas, the final formula would be

=If(Isnumber(Search(" -",B10)-1)=TRUE,Mid(B10,1,Search(" -",B10)-1),B10)

f. Delete columns C to E; then copy the formula in C10 to the whole data list.

	A	B	C
1	Co_Name	Industry_Class	
2	01 COMPUTER SYSTEM PTE LTD	Wholesale - Telecom / Office Apparatus / Computers	Wholesale
3	3COM ASIA PACIFIC RIM PTE LIMITED	Wholesale - Telecom / Office Apparatus / Computers	Wholesale
4	68 SYSTEMS & PROJECT ENGINEERING	Construction - Fittings / Fixtures	Construction
5	A & ONE PRECISION ENGINEERING PTE	Construction - Structural / Mechanical Engineering	Construction
6	A & P CO-ORDINATOR PTE LTD	Services - Printing / Publishing	Services
7	A.P. MOLLER SINGAPORE PTE. LTD*	Comm/Tpt/Storage - Transport - Marine	Comm/Tpt/Storage
8	AAA INTERNATIONAL PTE LTD	Wholesale - Electrical / Electronic	Wholesale
9	AAAS COM SOLUTION PTE LTD	Retail - Office Apparatus / Computer / Related Accessor	Retail
10	ASIA POWER CORPORATION LIMITED	Electricity / Gas / Water	Electricity / Gas / Water
11	AAF SINGAPORE PTE. LTD.	Mfg - Machinery / Equipment	Mfg
12	AAUT INDUSTRIES PTE LTD	Wholesale - Agricultural / Animal	Wholesale
...			
2649	ZHONGJING (SINGAPORE) OIL CO PTE	Wholesale - Solid / Liqu. / Gaseous Fuels and Related	Wholesale
2650	ZIRCON ENGINEERING PTE LTD	Wholesale - Electrical / Electronic	Wholesale
2651	ZUELLIG PHARMA PTE. LTD.	Wholesale - Medicinal / Pharmaceuticals Products	Wholesale
2652	ZURICH INSURANCE (SINGAPORE) PTE. L	Finance - Insurance / Re-insurance Services	Finance
2653			

3.4 Merge 2 lists into one using formulas

a. To transfer the industry class to the main list, use the (*f*x) *VLOOKUP* formula.

To use the (*f*x) *VLOOKUP* formula, there must a common value between the two tables. In this case, the company name is common between the 2 tables. Therefore, you must lookup the company name (referenced in **CoList** worksheet) and return the relevant results into the cell.

The (*f*x) *VLOOKUP* formula e.g =Vlookup(A2,IndustryClass!$A$2:$C$2652,3,FALSE)

contains 4 parts:

Part 1: The value to look up for. It can be a number, text, a cell reference or a formula. It is **A2** in our example.

Part 2: The range to find the lookup value. In our example, it is **$A$2:$C$2652** in **IndustryClass** worksheet. Do take note of the **$** before the columns and the rows. It is marked as absolute cell reference. This is to allow us to copy the formula down to the rest of the rows without making the range move together with the (*f*x) *VLOOKUP* formula.

Part 3: The value to return in the range (indicated in Part 2). In the range (IndustryClass!$A$2:$C$2652), we can indicate 1,2 or 3 because we have three columns (A to C). If **3** is used, it means that the (*f*x) *VLOOKUP* formula will return the value found in column 3 (on the same row where (*f*x) *VLOOKUP* formula found the value (reference to cell A2) in the range (IndustryClass!$A$2:$C$2652). If you use value more than 3, you will get an error because the range has only 3 columns. The more columns you indicate in the range, the more columns you can choose from. **BUT, YOU MUST READ THIS**! It will also increase your file size when you range more columns. So do not choose too many columns too. The word is BALANCE.

Part 4: I call this the switch. By default (meaning you omit the value), it is **TRUE**. This means that (*f*x) *VLOOKUP* formula will return a value closest to the lookup value if they are not able to find the EXACT value. For that to happen, your list must be organised in ascending order. What I always do is to set it to **FALSE**. This means that it will return the EXACT value. We want to have the most accurate data for our list. So remember to put in "FALSE" in Part 4.

b. Go to cell D2 of the **CoList** worksheet. In the cell, enter the (*fx*) *VLOOKUP* formula **=Vlookup(A2,IndustryClass!$A$2:$C$2652,3,FALSE)**. Copy the formula down for the whole list.

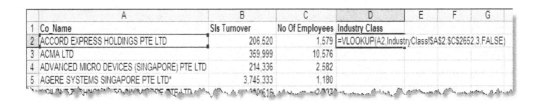

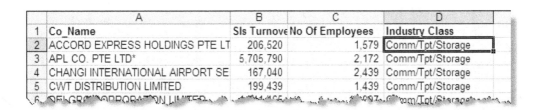

We are asking Excel to use the (*fx*) *VLOOKUP* formula to look up the company name which is in cell **A2**, in the range which lies in another worksheet, the **IndustryClass** worksheet. Note that the first column in the range must be the company name so that the formula can find a match. When Excel found the company name, return the result that is shown in column **3**. The **FALSE** is to instruct Excel to return the exact results. If (*fx*) *VLOOKUP* formula cannot find the value, it returns an error.

3.5 Create subtotals automatically for each category of data

a. Select one of the cells in the list. Go to Main Menu, select **Data → Sort**.

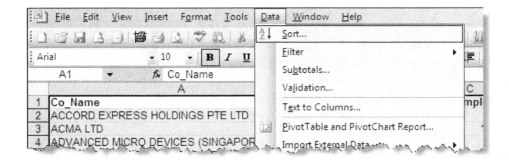

b. Re-sort the data based on industry class using the combined list.

We need to sort the data so that we could group the companies in the same industry class together for the purpose of calculating the industry class' subtotal.

c. Use **SUBTOTAL** function to calculate the number of companies in each industry class or the total sum of the turnover. This **SUBTOTAL** function is NOT THE SAME as the (**ƒx**) *SUBTOTAL* formula we saw in out earlier cases.

d. Go to Main Menu, select **Data → Subtotal**.

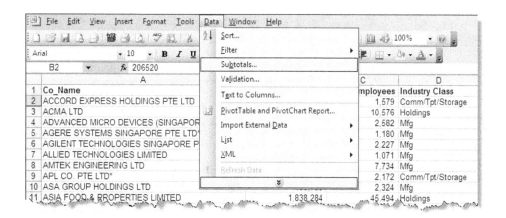

e. In the popup **Subtotal** box, select

    i. **Industry Class** from the dropdown list under the category **at every change in**.

    ii. **Sum** as the function to use;

    iii. Check the field(s) to add subtotal to based on the function (Sls Turnover and Industry Class)

    iv. Check on **Replace current subtotals** if it exists and **Summary below data** to put the subtotal results below the data.

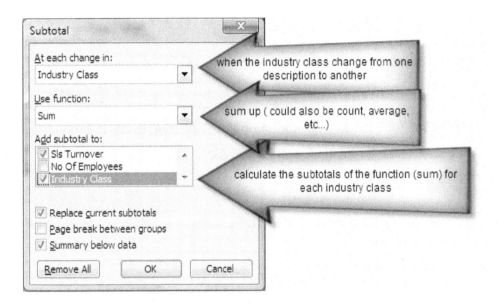

What does the above setting do?

The above setting is the instruction to **SUBTOTAL** function to check for changes in the industry class description. When detected a change, it will insert a subtotal on the number of records for that category (in this case - Industry Class). The option "**Replace current subtotals**" will replace any subtotal that was created previously. In our case, there is none to replace. Selecting the option "**Summary below data**" will present the subtotal below the records that added up the subtotal. If the box is not checked, the subtotal will be presented first followed by the details leading to the subtotal.

f. Once Excel has created the subtotal for the entire data list. Click on the number **2** on the top left column, it will hide the rows and display only the grand total and subtotals.

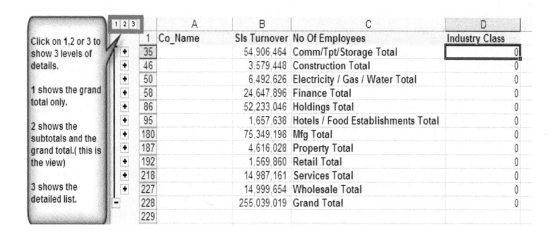

g. To count the number of companies in each industry class, replace the function number 9 by function number 3. Highlight the range D2:D228. Go to **Edit → Find**.

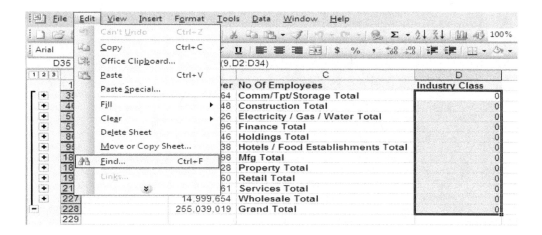

h. Enter **"(9,"** in Find what: panel. Click on the Replace tab and key in **"(3,"** in the Replace with: panel. The "**(**" and "**,**" is included to make the search more precise and specific. Click **Replace All**. You should have 12 replacements.

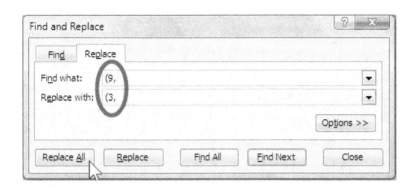

1 2		A	B	C	D
	1	Co_Name	Sls Turnover	No Of Employees	Industry Class
+	35		54,906,464	Comm/Tpt/Storage Total	33
+	46		3,579,448	Construction Total	10
+	50		6,492,626	Electricity / Gas / Water Total	3
+	58		24,647,896	Finance Total	7
+	86		52,233,046	Holdings Total	27
+	95		1,657,638	Hotels / Food Establishments Total	8
+	180		75,349,198	Mfg Total	84
+	187		4,616,028	Property Total	6
+	192		1,569,860	Retail Total	4
+	218		14,987,161	Services Total	25
+	227		14,999,654	Wholesale Total	8
−	228		255,039,019	Grand Total	215
	229				

3.6 Format all your subtotals at one go

a.   Use the **Go To** Function to highlight the subtotals in yellow; select the range **A1: D228**.

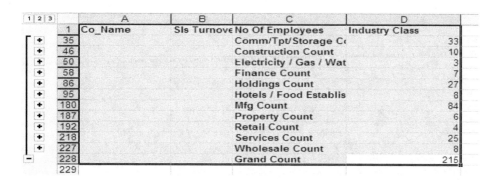

b.   Go to Main Menu and click on **Edit → Go To**. Alternatively, you could press the F5 key.

c.   Click on the **Special** button located at the bottom left corner.

d.   Select the option **Visible cells only** and click **OK**. This will highlight the visible cells only.

43

e.   Format the selected cells based on your preference. (e.g. highlight the cell with yellow)

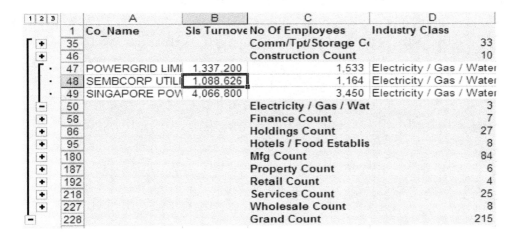

1 2 3		A	B	C	D	
	1	Co_Name	Sls Turnove	No Of Employees	Industry Class	
+	35			Comm/Tpt/Storage C(		33
+	46			Construction Count		10
+	50			Electricity / Gas / Wat		3
+	58			Finance Count		7
+	86			Holdings Count		27
+	95			Hotels / Food Establis		8
+	180			Mfg Count		84
+	187			Property Count		6
+	192			Retail Count		4
+	218			Services Count		25
+	227			Wholesale Count		8
-	228			Grand Count		215
	229					

f.   Click on number **3** on the top left hand corner of the worksheet, you should see the grand total and sub total rows highlighted.

1 2 3		A	B	C	D
	1	Co_Name	Sls Turnove	No Of Employees	Industry Class
+	35			Comm/Tpt/Storage C(	33
+	46			Construction Count	10
·	47	POWERGRID LIMI	1,337,200	1,533	Electricity / Gas / Water
·	48	SEMBCORP UTILI	1,088,626	1,164	Electricity / Gas / Water
·	49	SINGAPORE POW	4,066,800	3,450	Electricity / Gas / Water
-	50			Electricity / Gas / Wat	3
+	58			Finance Count	7
+	86			Holdings Count	27
+	95			Hotels / Food Establis	8
+	180			Mfg Count	84
+	187			Property Count	6
+	192			Retail Count	4
+	218			Services Count	25
+	227			Wholesale Count	8
-	228			Grand Count	215

44

3.7 List of Errors returned by Excel formulas

What Shows Up in the Cell	What's Going On Here?
#DIV/0!	When a number is divided by zero (0).
#NAME?	When Excel could not recognize the formula or the range name you entered into the formula
#NULL!	Appears most often when you insert a space (where you should have used a comma) to separate cell references used as arguments for functions.
#NUM!	Appears when Excel encounters a problem with a number in the formula, such as the wrong type of argument in an Excel function or a calculation that produces a number too large or too small to be represented in the worksheet.
#REF!	Appears when Excel encounters an invalid cell reference, such as when you delete a cell referred to in a formula or paste cells over the cells referred to in a formula.
#VALUE!	Appears when the formula expected to return a number returns an error.

Solution 3B

3.8 Separate text in a cell in 3 simple steps

> In this solution, we will use **Text to Column** function (In Lotus 1-2-3, it is known as parsing data) to retrieve the general industry class.

a. Highlight the range **B2:B2652** in the **IndustryClass** worksheet. Go to Main Menu, click on **Data → Text to Columns**.

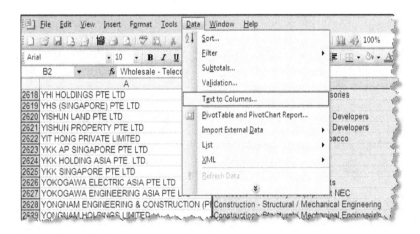

b. Select the **Delimited** option.

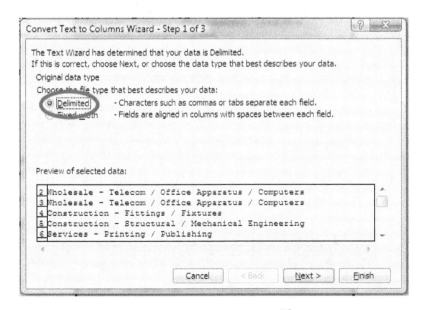

You can separate the text either by the **Delimited** option or by **Fixed width**. When you choose **Delimited**, Excel will separate the value by the delimiter you have chosen (could be a comma, semi-colon, etc). The commonly used delimiter is comma. If you open a csv (comma separated values) file in Excel, it will automatically separate the values into different fields using comma as a delimiter.

Fixed width is similar to the mid function we have used in Solution A. It will break up the text based on the number of characters. Using this option in our example will break up the industry class "construction" into construct if the width is 9 characters.

c.   Use "**-**" as the delimiter and click **Next>**.

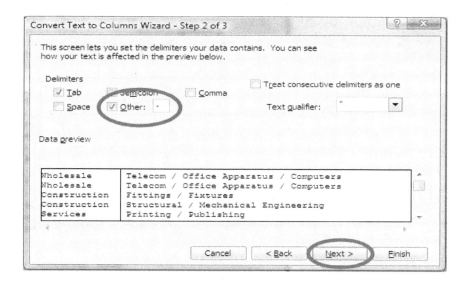

d. To prevent the result from being over-written, select a new destination to place the results. In our case, we select cell **C2** and click **Finished**.

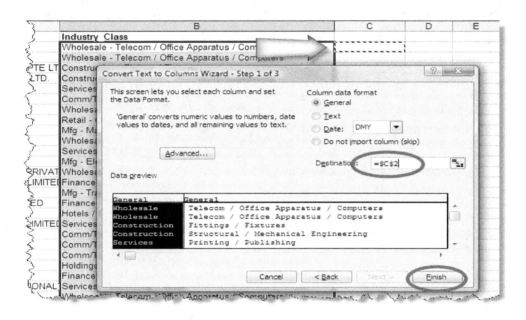

e. The final output is as such :

f. Try to merge the 2 lists into one on your own. (Hint: see solution 3.4.)

3.9 Remove duplicates in a list (Method 1)

We will not be using the **Subtotal** function like in solution 3.5. Instead, we will approach the case differently by presenting the summary below the data. Here is how:

a. Sort the delimited **IndustryClass** list according to column C in ascending order. Check on the **Header row** so that row 1 which consists of the header names will not be included in the sorting.

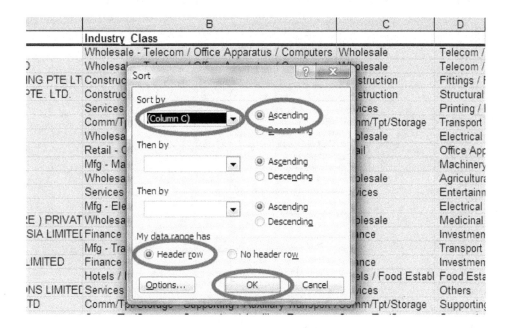

b. Copy the general industry classification (column C) to a new worksheet. Enter the header **Industry Class** into cell A1 and **Unique Records** into cell B1. In cell B2, enter the (f_x) *IF* formula **=If(A2=A1,"",A2)**.

c. Copy the formula down to the end of the list. Notice that some cells appeared to be blank.

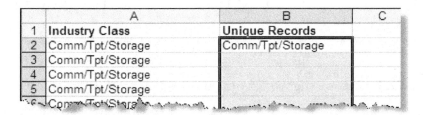

d. Select the **AutoFilter** function and filter to get only the **Non Blank** cells.

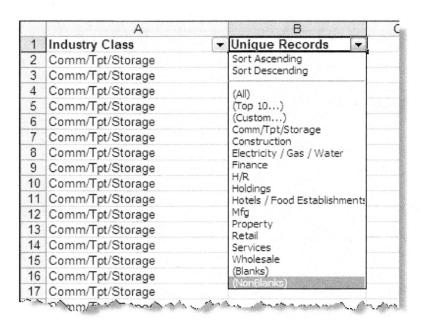

e.   Highlight the range under **Unique Records**. Use **GoTo** function, click **Special** and then select **Visible cells only.** Copy the list.

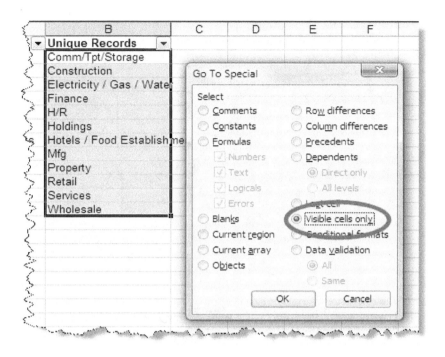

f.   Paste the listing onto rows below the data in **CoList** worksheet.

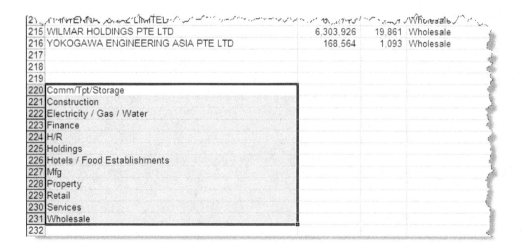

3.10 Remove duplicates using advanced filters (Method 2)

a.   Select the range you want to derive your unique records. In this case, highlight the range C2:C2652 in **IndustryClass** Worksheet.

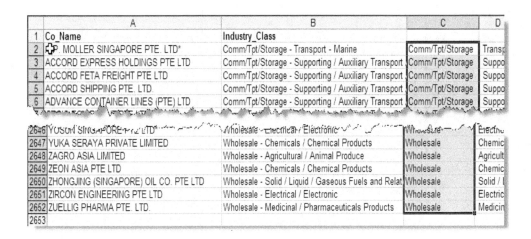

b.   Go to Main Menu, select **Data → Filter → Advanced Filter**.

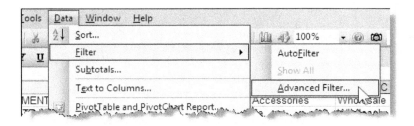

c. In the list range box, you will notice that it has been filed in with the selected range. Select the option: **Copy to another location**.

d. Make sure that the **Criteria range** input box is empty. In the **Copy to** box, enter the cell you want to present your results (Note that you can only copy the filtered data in the active/same sheet). Check on the box **Unique records only**. Click **OK**.

3.11 Find averages

> Use the (fx) SUMIF formula to find the total revenue and total number of employees for each industry. To get average, divide (fx) SUMIF by (fx) COUNTIF.

a. Enter the (fx) SUMIF formula [=sumif($D$2:$D$216,A220,$B$2:$B$216)] in cell B220 to find the total revenue for each category.

213	PUTRA PRODUCTS PTE LTD	14,405	29,4	Wholesale
214	TT INTERNATIONAL LIMITED	652,713	1,127	Wholesale
215	WILMAR HOLDINGS PTE LTD	6,303,926	19,861	Wholesale
216	YOKOGAWA ENGINEERING ASIA PTE LTD	168,564	1,093	Wholesale
217				
218				
219				
220	Comm/Tpt/Storage	=SUMIF($D$2:$D$216,A220,$B$2:$B$216)		
221	Construction			
222	Electricity / Gas / Water			
223	Finance			
224	H/R			

b. Copy the formula down the rest of the industry class list; enter the (fx) SUMIF formula [=sumif($D$2:$D$216,A220,$B$2:$B$216)] in cell C220 to find the total number of employees for each category.

...	...goods...	414,3	29,4	Wholesale
214	TT INTERNATIONAL LIMITED	652,713	1,127	Wholesale
215	WILMAR HOLDINGS PTE LTD	6,303,926	19,861	Wholesale
216	YOKOGAWA ENGINEERING ASIA PTE LTD	168,564	1,093	Wholesale
217				
218				
219				
220	Comm/Tpt/Storage	54,906,464	=SUMIF($D$2:$D$216,A220,$C$2:$C$216)	
221	Construction	3,579,448		
222	Electricity / Gas / Water	6,492,626		
223	Finance	24,647,896		
224	H/R	0		

c. Copy the formula down the rest of the industry class list; enter the (fx) COUNTIF formula [=countif($C$2:$C$216,A220)] in cell D220 to find the number of companies in each category.

214	TT INTERNATIONAL LIMITED	652,713	1,127	Wholesale
215	WILMAR HOLDINGS PTE LTD	6,303,926	19,861	Wholesale
216	YOKOGAWA ENGINEERING ASIA PTE LTD	168,564	1,093	Wholesale
217				
218				
219				
220	Comm/Tpt/Storage	54,906,464	185,801	=countif($D$2:$D$216,A220)
221	Construction	3,579,448	19,560	
222	Electricity / Gas / Water	6,492,626	6,147	
223	Finance	24,647,896	40,508	

d.   To get average, divide (ƒx) **SUMIF** by (ƒx) **COUNTIF**.

214	TT INTERNATIONAL LIMITED	652,713	1,127	Wholesale	
215	WILMAR HOLDINGS PTE LTD	6,303,926	19,861	Wholesale	
216	YOKOGAWA ENGINEERING ASIA PTE LTD	168,564	1,093	Wholesale	
217					
218					
219					
220	Comm/Tpt/Storage	54,906,464	185,801	33	+B220/D220
221	Construction	3,579,448	19,560	10	
222	Electricity / Gas / Water	6,492,626	6,147	3	
223	Finance	24,647,896	40,508	7	

214	TT INTERNATIONAL LIMITED	652,713	1,127	Wholesale		
215	WILMAR HOLDINGS PTE LTD	6,303,926	19,861	Wholesale		
216	YOKOGAWA ENGINEERING ASIA PTE LTD	168,564	1,093	Wholesale		
217						
218						
219						
220	Comm/Tpt/Storage	54,906,464	185,801	33	1,663,832.24	+C220/D220
221	Construction	3,579,448	19,560	10	357,944.80	
222	Electricity / Gas / Water	6,492,626	6,147	3	2,164,208.67	
223	Finance	24,647,896	40,508	7	3,521,128.00	

					Ave Revenue	Ave no. Of employees
218						
219						
220	Comm/Tpt/Storage	54,906,464	185,801	33	1,663,832.24	5,630.33
221	Construction	3,579,448	19,560	10	357,944.80	1,956.00
222	Electricity / Gas / Water	6,492,626	6,147	3	2,164,208.67	2,049.00
223	Finance	24,647,896	40,508	7	3,521,128.00	5,786.86
224	H/R	0	0	0	#DIV/0!	#DIV/0!
225	Holdings	52,233,046	277,451	27	1,934,557.26	10,275.96
226	Hotels / Food Establishments	1,657,638	18,393	8	207,204.75	2,299.13
227	Mfg	75,349,198	370,054	84	897,014.26	4,405.40
228	Property	4,616,028	11,336	6	769,338.00	1,889.33
229	Retail	1,569,860	7,696	4	392,465.00	1,924.00
230	Services	14,987,161	88,429	25	599,486.44	3,537.16
231	Wholesale	14,999,654	39,535	8	1,874,956.75	4,941.88
232						

End of Case 3

Tips and Tricks 4

Entering value / text / formula at various cells all at one go

When we are working on our worksheet, we have this tendency to select the cells that require a certain formula. Then we realise that we can only enter the formula cell by cell. How can we then enter the formula all at one go without having to reselect the cells again?

1. Highlight the cells that you wish to enter the same value / text / formulas in. Type in the value / text / formula. In this example, we type in **enter all at one go**.

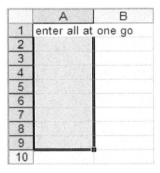

2. Use **Ctrl** key + **Enter** key. The rest of the cells are copied with the same text.

	A	B
1	enter all at	one go
2	enter all at	one go
3	enter all at	one go
4	enter all at	one go
5	enter all at	one go
6	enter all at	one go
7	enter all at	one go
8	enter all at	one go
9	enter all at	one go
10		

CASE

Case 4:   Pivot Table unveiled

Key Learning Points: Create Pivot Table using an Excel range.

Case Study:

Your customers have been complaining that too many of your salesmen are visiting them and they are confused as to who to contact for an enquiry. Because of this, the company was not able to build a strong relationship with the customer. You are told to identify the salesmen that have been selling products to a particular customer and to reduce the point of contact to one sales person. You are told to assign the customer to the sales person who has the most dealing with the customer in terms of sales.

	A	B	C	D	E	F
1	✚ Customer Name	DO No.	DO Date	Slsman No	Promotion?	Mat'l Part No.
2	JVC ELECTRONICS SINGAPORE PTE. LTD.	20901001NVY	9/3/95	9	no	Part No 31
3	ASPIAL CORPORATION LIMITED	20901002YCM	9/5/95	4	No	Part No 764
4	CHEMICAL INDUSTRIES (FAR EAST) LIMITED.	20901004YCM	9/5/95	4	No	Part No 175
5	AVX/KYOCERA HOLDINGS PTE. LTD.	20901002YCM	9/5/95	4	No	Part No 753
6	KIM ENG SECURITIES PTE. LTD.	20901005YVY	9/5/95	9	No	Part No 813
7	KOCH REFINING INTERNATIONAL PTE. LTD.	20901003YCM	9/5/95	4	No	Part No 580
8	NATIONAL UNIVERSITY HOSPITAL (SINGAPORE) PTE LTD	20901006VY	9/5/95	9	No	Part No 258
9	NJR (SINGAPORE) PTE LTD	20901006VY	9/5/95	9	No	Part No 258
10	PEARSON EDUCATION SOUTH ASIA PTE. LTD.	20901002YCM	9/5/95		No	Part No 762

Pivot table is one of the greatest functions ever to be incorporated into Excel. It has the functionalities of specialised reporting tools such as business objects, crystal report, impromptu, etc. Its drag and drop feature allow you to organise and present data quickly. And it works with an Excel worksheet, Access databases, Dbase and even database servers.

Personally, I prefer to work with Pivot tables because I could do more with it. But I am sure there are some who feels that certain reports best prepared using the **SUBTOTAL** function.

Working File:

1.   *4.Pivot Table unveiled.xls*
2.   *4.Pivot Table unveiled-soln.xls*

Solution:

4.1   Create a pivot table using data from a Excel spreadsheet

a.   Select a cell within the data list. Go to Main Menu and select **Data -> PivotTable and PivotChart Report**.

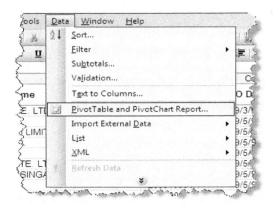

b.   Select the **Microsoft Office Excel list or database** option and **Pivot Table** option and click **Next>**.

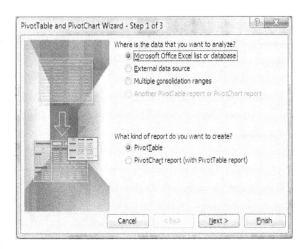

c.   Highlight the range of data that the pivot table would be based on.

Excel will auto detect the range to use as data source for the pivot table. It is important to check that the range is correct. Excel may not capture all the rows if there is a break in between the records.

d.   When you come to the wizard step 3 of 3, click on **Layout** button.

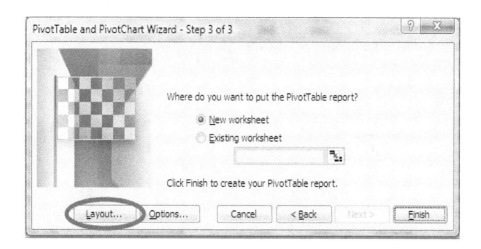

e.   ***Drag and drop*** the fields into the respective places as shown below and click **OK**.

Note: For the rest of this document, we will use the term "drag and drop" as a short form for the action
Point the cursor at the item (e.g. Customer), click and hold and move (this will move the item) to the designated area. Drop the item into the designated area by releasing the mouse button.

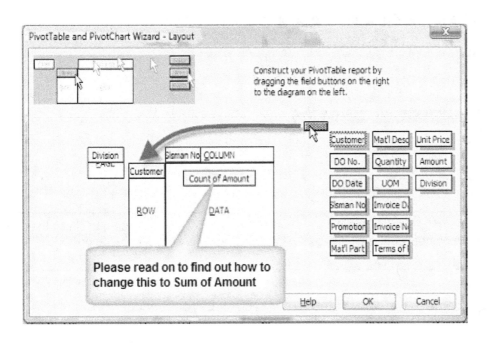

To change the Count of Amount to Sum of Amount:
Double click on Count of Amount. The Select Sum in the "**Summarize by**" box.

Click OK. The pivot table will now Sum up the amount instead of counting the number of records in each category.

f. Select **New worksheet** option and click **Finish**.

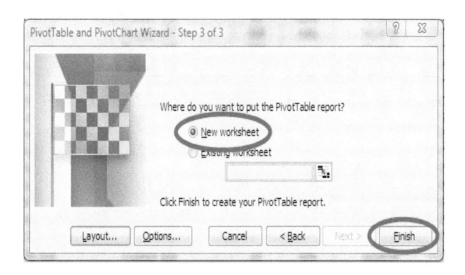

g. This is how the data is presented when you drag and drop the item into the different places in the layout segment.

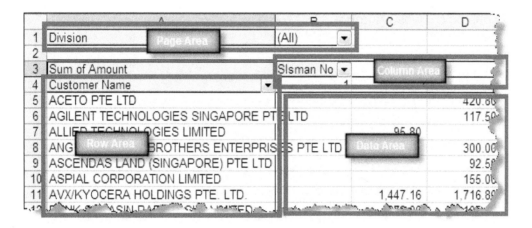

4.2   Format the Pivot Table

Besides formatting the Pivot Table at the **Layout** popup box, you may also format the Pivot Table In its report view.

a.   To format the **Sum of Amount** results in the **Data Area**, double click on the grey Box called **Sum of Amount**.

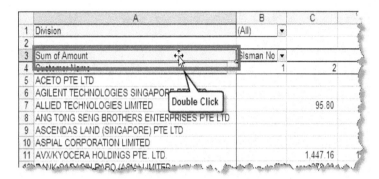

b.   In the popup box, choose **Number**.

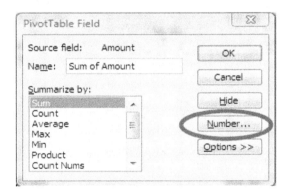

c. Format the number as shown below and click **OK** twice to close the two boxes.

d. Double click on the grey box **Customer Name** to arrange the customer in descending order of purchases

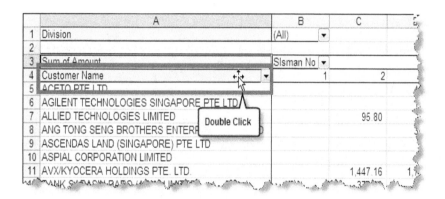

e. Select the **Advanced** button.

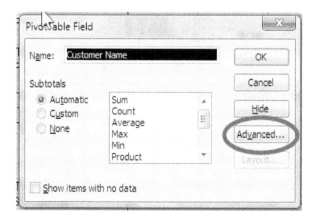

f.   Under the **AutoSort** Option, check on **Descending** to arrange the Customer Name in descending order using the sum of amount as a basis. In the **Using Field**, select **Sum of Amount** and click **OK** twice to close the boxes.

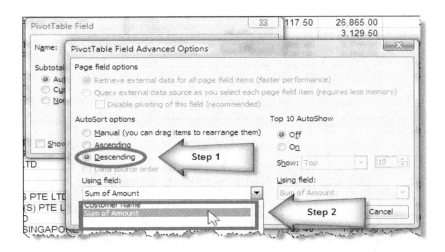

g.   The Pivot Table changes to show the Customers' Sales Amount in descending order.

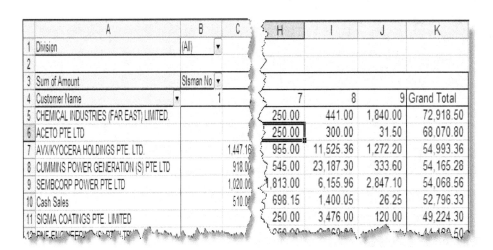

4.3   Change the pivot table layout in report view

a.   Re-arrange the results such that we could analyse the customer in further details; drag and hold the **Slsman No** field and move it next to the **Customer Name** field. Drop it (release the hold) when you see the dotted line appears.

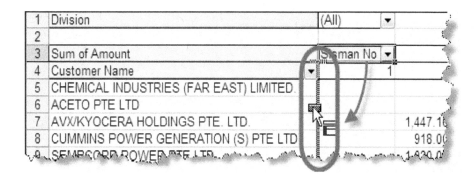

b. Given below is what you should get:

	A	B	C
1	Division	(All)	
2			
3	Sum of Amount		
4	Customer Name	Slsman No	Total
5	CHEMICAL INDUSTRIES (FAR EAST) LIMITED.	3	414.50
6		4	69,423.00
7		6	550.00
8		7	250.00
9		8	441.00
10		9	1,840.00
11	CHEMICAL INDUSTRIES (FAR EAST) LIMITED. Total		72,918.50
12	ACETO PTE LTD	3	420.80
13		4	59,956.70
14		5	114.00
15		6	6,997.80
		7	250.00

4.4 Sort the list based on the results

a. Do a auto sort by descending order on "**Slsman No**" using field "**Sum of Amount**". Double click on **Slsman No** grey box, select the **Advanced** button.

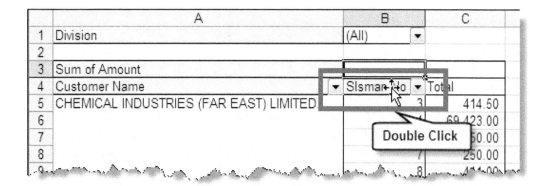

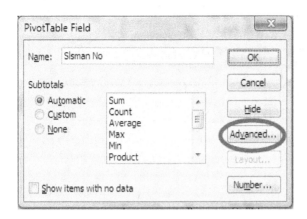

b. Under the **AutoSort** Option, check on **Descending** to arrange the Salesman number in descending order using the sum of amount as a basis. In the **Using Field**, select **Sum of Amount** and click **OK** twice to close the boxes.

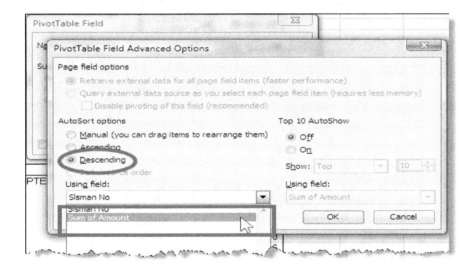

c. The Salesman number is sorted according to the highest sales amount transacted with the customer.

	A	B	C
1	Division	(All) ▼	
2			
3	Sum of Amount		
4	Customer Name ▼	Slsman No ▼	Total
5	CHEMICAL INDUSTRIES (FAR EAST) LIMITED.	4	69,423.00
6		9	1,840.00
7		6	550.00
8		8	441.00
9		3	414.50
10		7	250.00
11	CHEMICAL INDUSTRIES (FAR EAST) LIMITED. Total		72,918.50
12	ACETO PTE LTD	4	59,956.70

4.5 Display the top results only

a. Double click on the **Slsman No** grey box again. Click on **Advanced** and switch on **Top 10 AutoShow**. Show only **Top 1** using **Sum of Amount**. Select **OK** twice to close the boxes.

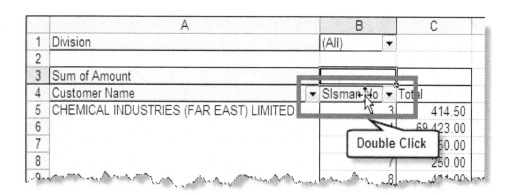

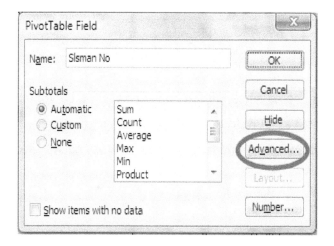

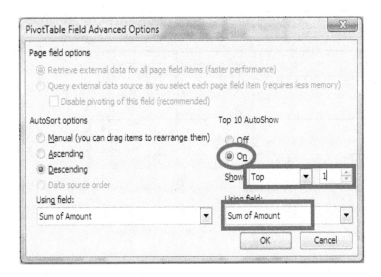

b. The result is as shown below, notice the **Slsman No** is displayed in bold blue to show that some results are hidden.

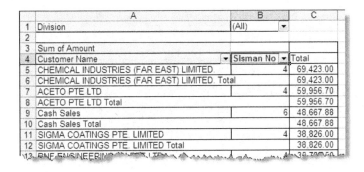

You can also choose bottom 10 if you want to see those customers who made the lowest purchases.

4.6 Hide the subtotals

a. Remove the subtotal for customer name since we are only displaying a customer and a salesman who has sold the highest amount to the customer. To do so, double click on **Customer Name** again. In the popup box, under **Subtotals** section, select **None** and click **OK**.

68

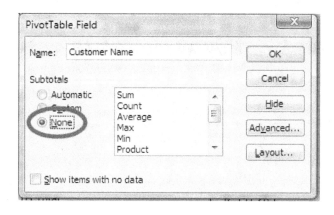

b. This final list will show you which salesman should continue to manage the relevant customer account.

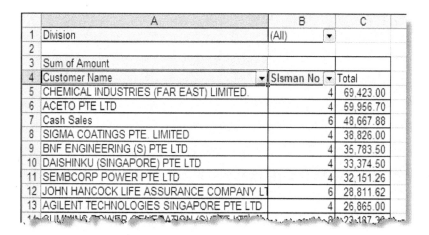

	A	B	C
1	Division	(All) ▼	
2			
3	Sum of Amount		
4	Customer Name ▼	Slsman No ▼	Total
5	CHEMICAL INDUSTRIES (FAR EAST) LIMITED.	4	69,423.00
6	ACETO PTE LTD	4	59,956.70
7	Cash Sales	6	48,667.88
8	SIGMA COATINGS PTE. LIMITED	4	38,826.00
9	BNF ENGINEERING (S) PTE LTD	4	35,783.50
10	DAISHINKU (SINGAPORE) PTE LTD	4	33,374.50
11	SEMBCORP POWER PTE LTD	4	32,151.26
12	JOHN HANCOCK LIFE ASSURANCE COMPANY LT	6	28,811.62
13	AGILENT TECHNOLOGIES SINGAPORE PTE LTD	4	26,865.00
14	GUMINING POWER GENERATION (S) PTE LTD	3	23,187.30

End of Case 4

Case 5: Format Pivot Table with Colours

Key Learning Points: Formatting the Pivot Table.

Case Study:

Continued from Case 4, you wish to further enhance your pivot table so that it looks colourful yet professional. Let's try to format the pivot table to make it more readable and attractive.

Working File:

1.   *4.Pivot Table unveiled-soln.xls*

Solution:

5.1 Format the entire pivot table with the right colour and font

a.   Place your cursor at the top left corner of the pivot table and click to highlight the entire pivot table.

	A	B	C
1	Division	(All) ▼	
2			
3	Sum of Amount		
4	Customer Name ▼	Slsman No ▼	Total
5	CHEMICAL INDUSTRIES (FAR EAST) LIMITED.	4	69,423.00
6		9	1,840.00
7		6	550.00
8		8	441.00
9		3	414.50
10		7	250.00
11	ACETO PTE LTD	4	59,956.70
12		6	6,997.80
13		3	420.80
14		8	300.00

b. Format the pivot table; you can change the font, font size, area colour and the font colour based on your preference.

5.2 Format the Columns

a. Place your cursor slight above the row name and click to highlight the first column.

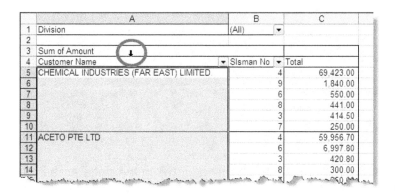

b. Format the column with your own reference. Repeat for the next few columns.

5.3 Format the Column Headers

a. Move the **Division** field and drop it at the Column area.

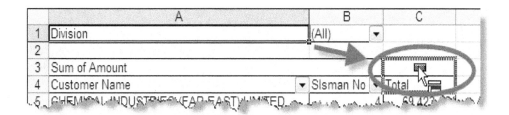

71

b.   Place your cursor slightly above the column name and click to highlight the header.

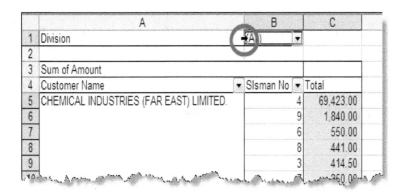

c.   Format the column header with your preference

5.4 Format the Data Area

a.   Place your cursor to the left of the value on any of items in the page area and click.

	A	B	C
1	Division	(A)	
2			
3	Sum of Amount		
4	Customer Name	Slsman No	Total
5	CHEMICAL INDUSTRIES (FAR EAST) LIMITED.	4	69,423.00
6		9	1,840.00
7		6	550.00
8		8	441.00
9		3	414.50

b.   Format the Data area as you like.

5.5 Format the Subtotals for the rows.

a.   Place your cursor to the left of any one of the subtotal and click.

	A	B	C
1	Division	(All) ▼	
2			
3	Sum of Amount		
4	Customer Name ▼	Slsman No ▼	Total
5	CHEMICAL INDUSTRIES (FAR EAST) LIMITED.	4	69,423.00
6		9	1,840.00
7		6	550.00
8		8	441.00
9		3	414.50
10		7	250.00
11	CHEMICAL INDUSTRIES (FAR EAST) LIMITED. Total		72,918.50
12	ACETO PTE LTD	4	59,956.70
13		6	6,997.80
14		3	420.80
15		8	300.00
16		7	250.00
17		5	114.00
18		9	31.50
19	ACETO PTE LTD Total		68,070.80
20	AVONKY SINA HOLDINGS PTE LTD		31,105.99

b.   Format the subtotals as you like.

End of Case 5

Case 6: Capture the format of the pivot table

Key Learning Points: Re use your favourite Pivot Table style.

Case Study:

Continued from Case 5, you want to save the formatted style created so that you can reuse it in the future. This will save you considerable time when you create new pivot tables. You could apply the same format repeatedly.

Working File:

1.   *4.Pivot Table unveiled-soln.xls*

Solution:

6.1   Preparation to capture the style you want

a.   Right click at the toolbar area and select **Customize**.

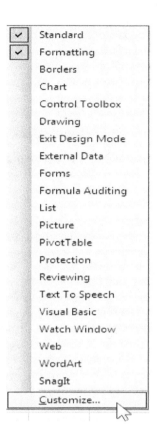

b.   Under **the Commands** Tab, select **Format** category, then select **Style** on the right side of the dialog box called **Commands**.

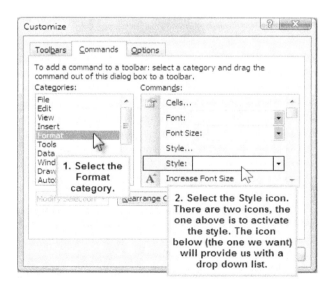

c.   Click on to the **Style** icon, drag it to the formatting toolbar and place it in the toolbar area. Click **Close** on the dialog box.

6.2 Capture the style we want in one step.

a.   Select a cell that contains the formatting we want to re-use for other ranges. Click on the style selection box and type in a name for style. In our case, type in **Pivot_All** and hit the 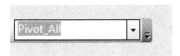 key.

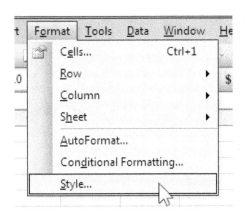

b.   To check on the style we have defined, go to Main Menu and click **Format → Style**.

c. Select the style name (**Pivot_All**) we want to check.

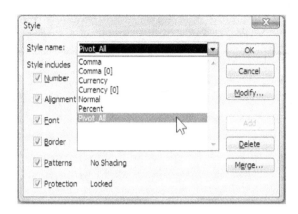

d. The Style (Pivot_All) will list down the format of the cell we have captured. Click Modify to change if needed. You can turn off one or more of the formats by checking off the box on the left of the format.

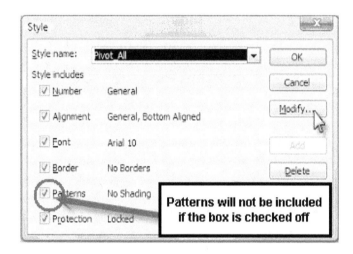

Patterns will not be included if the box is checked off

e. To apply the style, highlight the area and select **Pivot_All** style from the **Style** icon. The area will be formatted according to the style set.

End of Case 6

Tips and Tricks 5

Double click on the Format Painter icon.

Format Painter

If you double click on the paint brush icon, you can use it multiple times and at non continuous cells.

	A	B	C	D	E	
1						
2						
3						
4					✚🧹	
5						
6						
7						
8						
9						
10						
11						
12						
13						
14						
15						

Case 7: Use MS Query in Pivot Tables

Key Learning Points: Create Pivot Table using MS Query.

Case Study:

Your customers have been complaining that too many of your salesmen are visiting them and they are confused as to who to contact for an enquiry. Because of this, the company was not able to build a strong relationship with the customer. You are told to identify the salesmen that have been selling products to a particular customer and to reduce the point of contact to one sales person. You are told to assign the customer to the sales person who has the most dealing with the customer in terms of sales.

	A	B	C	D	E	F	
1	Customer Name	DO No.	DO Date	Slsman No	Promotion?	Mat'l Part No	Mat'l
2	JVC ELECTRONICS SINGAPORE PTE. LTD.	20901001NVY	9/3/95	9	no	6040	Adhesive Re
3	ASPIAL CORPORATION LIMITED	20901002YCM	9/5/95	4	No	Senisui Paper	Size: 4
4	CHEMICAL INDUSTRIES (FAR EAST) LIMITED.	20901004YCM	9/5/95	4	No	1015	Cushion Mo
5	AVX/KYOCERA HOLDINGS PTE. LTD.	20901002YCM	9/5/95	4	No	Daiichi Cellulose	Size: 1
6	KIM ENG SECURITIES PTE. LTD.	20901005YVY	9/5/95	9	No	1345	Tape Adh Ta
7	KOCH REFINING INTERNATIONAL PTE. LTD.	20901003YCM	9/5/95	4	No	5421	Polyethyle
8	NATIONAL UNIVERSITY HOSPITAL (SINGAPORE) PTE LTD	20901006VY	9/5/95	9	No	4950	Double Sided
9	NJR (SINGAPORE) PTE LTD	20901006VY	9/5/95	9	No	4950	Double Sided
10	PEARSON EDUCATION SOUTH ASIA PTE. LTD.	20901002YCM	9/5/95	4	No	Acebond Box	Size: 48
11	SPORTS NETWORK PTE LTD	20901002YCM	9/5		No		

Note that this case is identical to Case 4 except that in this case, we use MS query to create the pivot table.

79

About MS Query

MS Query is a simple but powerful ad-hoc query tool that you can use to retrieve and organize data from databases (such as Access, SQL database server, Dbase, or even Excel worksheets, just to name a few). The retrieved data can be displayed directly in a MS Excel worksheet for further editing or be presented in a pivot table, pivot chart report or just as list of records.

The feature is readily available in MSOffice but not installed in the standard setup. To check whether this function is installed in your computer, please refer to Appendix 1.

Working File:

1. *7.Use MS query in Pivot tables.xls*
2. *7.Use MS query in Pivot tables-soln.xls*

Solution:

7.1 Create pivot table using data stored in a database

In our case, we make use of another Excel workbook to mimic a database. You can actually use exactly the same method to access a MS Access database, SQL database server, dbase, etc.

    a.   Open a brand new workbook. At the Main Menu, select **Data → PivotTable and PivotChart Report**.

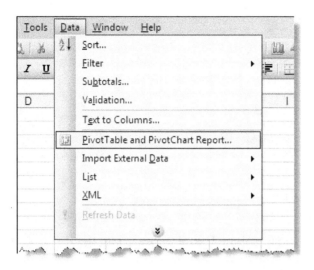

b.   Select **External Data Source** option and **Pivot Table** option; click **Next>**.

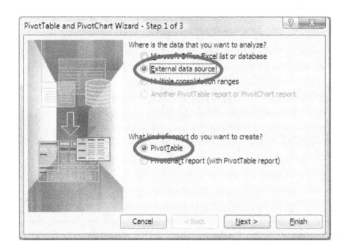

c.   Click on the **Get Data** Button.

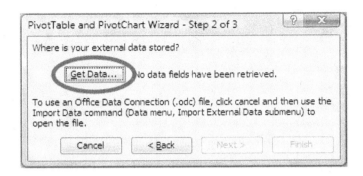

d.   In the **Choose Data Source** popup box, select **Excel Files***. Uncheck the **Use the Query Wizard to create/edit queries** option. Click **OK**.

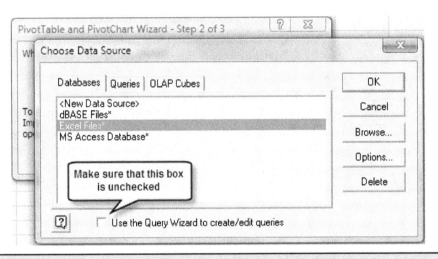

In our example, we select Excel Files as the data source because the data is stored in Excel Workbooks. You can use the same method to access dBase Files, MS Access and for some of you SQL databases (SQL database are database servers which is used to stored huge amount of records, most probably in the millions.

Also, please make sure that the **Use the Query Wizard to create/edit queries** option is unchecked. This is more of my personal preference. I find that it is easier to work with the query on my own than to use the wizard. After you have learnt my method, you can always come back to try out how the wizard works.

e. Select the source Excel file, in this case, the file name is **Use Ms Query in pivot tables.xls**. Click **OK**.

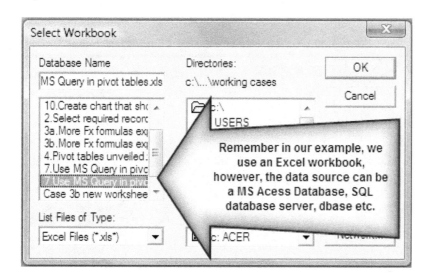

f. On the **Add Tables** popup box, select **Sheet1$** and click **Add**. Click **Close** to close the box.

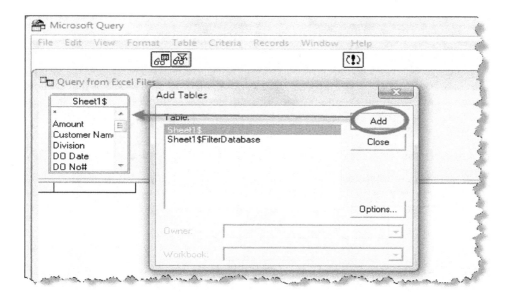

If you get the following dialog box with no file names appearing in it, click on the **Options** button;

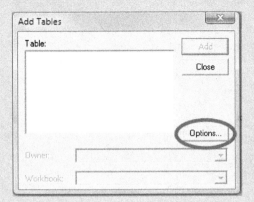

And check on **System Tables** option shown below and click **OK**.

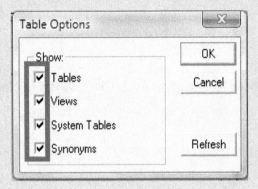

When you are at the **Add Table** popup box, you may see 2 names that look the same except that one comes with an underscore/extended name. Ignore the name with the underscore/extended name as it does not contain any details.

The table name is the same as the worksheet name, except for the "$" behind the name. This is how **MSQuery** present the worksheets as a database table.

g.   You can extend the box by placing the cursor on the right side of the table, when the double sided arrow appears, click and hold and move to the right.

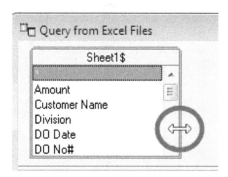

h.   There are 3 ways to select the fields to display in your Excel worksheet.

    i.   Find the field e.g. **Customer Name** and double click on it.

    ii.   Select the field **Customer Name**, drag and drop the name into the area below the table.

    iii. Click at the inverted arrow of the empty panel to display a list of the fields, select the field required.

Method 1 & 2

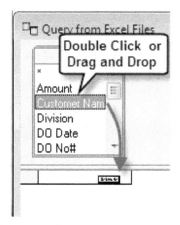

Method 3

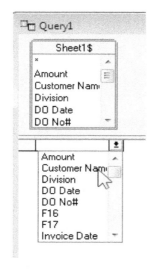

i. Repeat the same process for field names: **Salesman No**, **Amount**, **Division**, and **Terms of Payment**. Then, click on the **Return Data** icon to return to Excel.

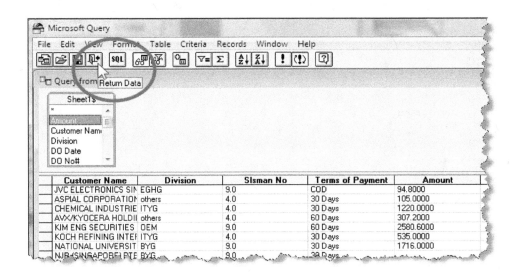

j. Alternatively, go to Main Menu and select **File → Return Data to Microsoft Office Excel**.

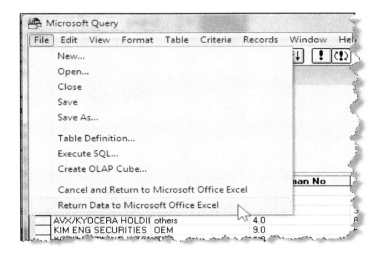

k.   In the step 2 of 3 of the Wizard, Next to the "**Get Data**" button, the description will change to "Data fields have been retrieved". Select **Next>**.

l.   Continue with the Wizard - Step 3 of 3, click on **Layout** button.

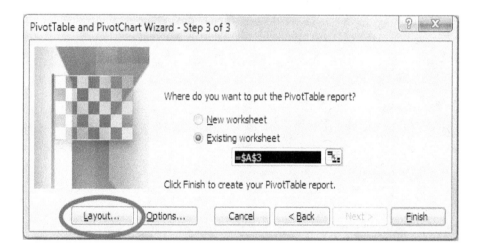

m.	Drag and drop the fields into the respective places as shown below and click **OK**.

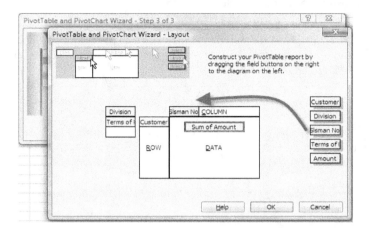

n.	Select the option to put the pivot Table on **a New worksheet** and click **Finish**.

o.	Bring the **Slsman No** to the right side of the **Customer Name**. Now you have the end result like case 4.

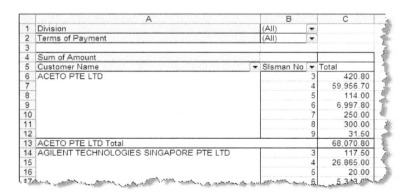

7.2 Update the Pivot table automatically at regular interval

Since the pivot table is drawing data from a database, it is highly possible that there are other users (and could be more than one user) who are writing records to database. By creating the pivot table using MSQuery, you are able to get updates from the database at regular interval. And you do not face the same problem as in case 4 where you need to re-size the data list to include the new records. (Unless you add in the new records one line before the last or use dynamic ranges).

    a.   Right click within the pivot table, a popup menu will appear. Select **Table Options**.

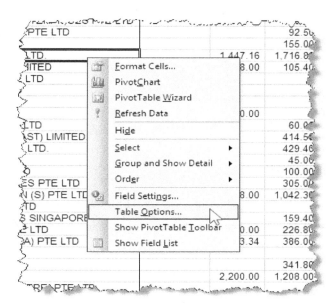

b. In the popup box, check on the **Refresh every x minutes** option. Click **OK**.

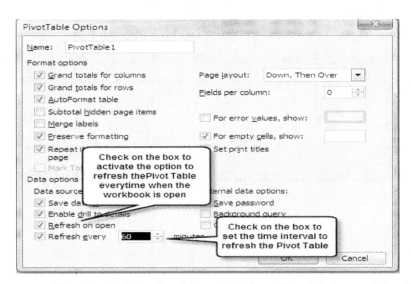

c. The pivot table will retrieve data from the database at the time interval you have set and refresh the pivot table with the updated information.

7.3 Hide the details for the rows description

a. Move your cursor over to the top of the row until you see the black arrow pointing downward. Make sure the black arrow is just above the row label. Click and you should see the rows highlighted.

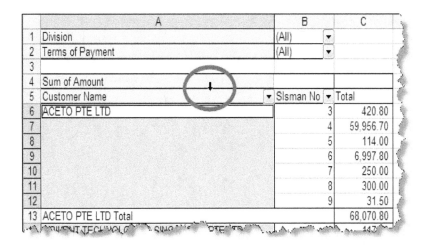

b. Move your cursor within the highlighted area and click. In the popup menu, click on **Group and Show Detail → Hide Detail**.

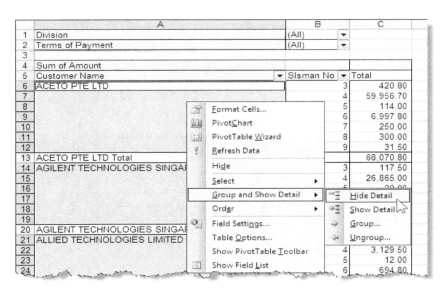

c. The salesman numbers are now all hidden, displaying only the customers' name.

	A	B		C
1	Division	(All)	▼	
2	Terms of Payment	(All)	▼	
3				
4	Sum of Amount			
5	Customer Name ▼	Slsman No	▼	Total
6	ACETO PTE LTD			68,070.80
7	AGILENT TECHNOLOGIES SINGAPORE PTE LTD			32,796.10
8	ALLIED TECHNOLOGIES LIMITED			19,606.50
9	ANG TONG SENG BROTHERS ENTERPRISES PTE LTD			9,625.70
10	ASCENDAS LAND (SINGAPORE) PTE LTD			12,995.61
11	ASPIAL CORPORATION LIMITED			23,879.25
12	AVX/KYOCERA HOLDINGS PTE. LTD.			54,993.36
13	BANK SARASIN-RABO (ASIA) LIMITED			6,568.10

7.4   Format the Subtotals like cell formatting

a.   You can format the subtotals like a cell with your preferred font, colour, style, etc.

b.   Move your cursor to the extreme left of the subtotal until you see a black arrow pointing to the right. Make sure you do not move the cursor to the row label as this will select the entire row instead. Click and all the subtotal rows will be highlighted.

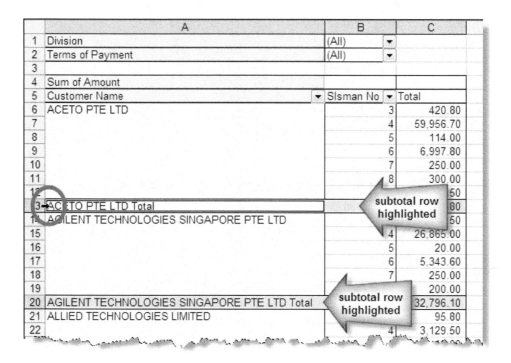

c.   Format the subtotal the way you would format the cells.

7.5 Present the details that make up the number in the data area

a.   Move your cursor over the number in the data area which you want to see the details and double click. Excel will insert a new worksheet and present the details in it. The pivot table still remains in the original worksheet.

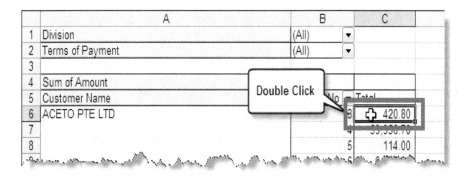

	A	B	C
1	Division	(All) ▼	
2	Terms of Payment	(All) ▼	
3			
4	Sum of Amount		
5	Customer Name	No	Total
6	ACETO PTE LTD		✚ 420.80
7			33,330.70
8		5	114.00

	A	B	C	D	E
1	Amount	Customer Name	Division	Slsman No	Terms of Payment
2	170	ACETO PTE LTD	BYG	3	30 Days
3	250.8	ACETO PTE LTD	EGHG	3	COD
4					
5					

Double Click

End of Case 7

Case 8: Database that has more rows than an Excel worksheet

Key Learning Points: Use of Auto Filter in MS Query

Case Study:

Assuming that the database in Case 7 has lots more rows that it could not display all rows in an Excel worksheet. We will use MS Query to help us to filter the records such that data list is reduced before it is imported to the Excel Worksheet.

Working File:

1.   *8.Database that has more rows than Excel Worksht.xls*
2.   *8.Database that has more rows than Excel Worksht-soln.xls*

Solution:

8.1   Auto filter in MS Query

MS Query has a filter function that will allow you to filter records so that the number of records to return to Excel can be reduced. This will reduce the Excel file size and possibly the memory required to generate the pivot table.

a.   Follow the step a to step h in case 7.1 to arrive at the diagram below. Click on the **Show/Hide Criteria** icon (indicated by the arrow) in the diagram below.

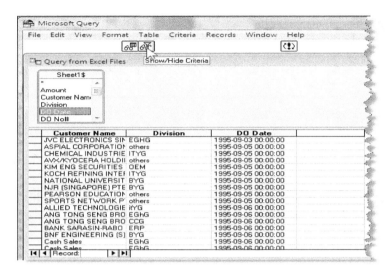

b. MS Query will present another section between the table and the data. This section will allow you to filter the records you want to retrieve from your database. Assuming that you are interested to look at the data from division **BYG**.

c. Click and drag the fieldname **Division** in **Sheet1$**, drop it into the **Criteria Field**. Or click in the first **Criteria Field**, a dropdown arrow at the left side will appear. Click on the arrow and select **Division** from the list.

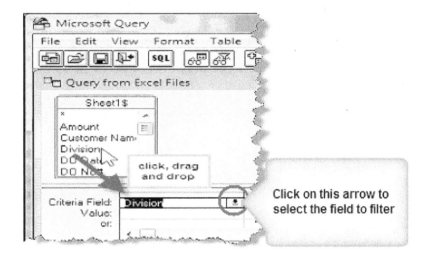

d.   Double click at the **Value** field.

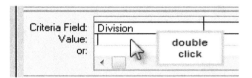

e.   When the **Edit Criteria** dialog box appears, click on the **Values** button.

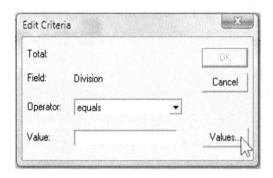

f.   Select the value **BYG** from the dialog box and click **OK**. Click **OK** again to close the
      Edit Criteria dialog box.

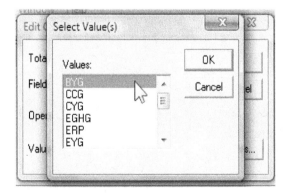

g. MS Query now presents the data that contains the word **BYG** in the division field name.

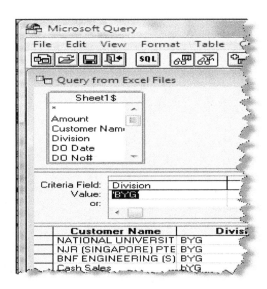

h. You can filter more data by adding more criteria by repeating step c to step g. You can vary the conditions by selecting the operator you want from the drop down box in the **Edit Criteria** dialog box.

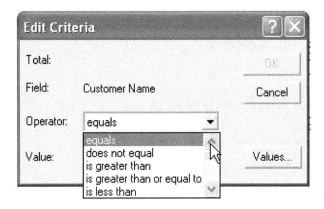

i. Return the data to Excel by clicking on the **Return Data** icon or select **Return Data to Microsoft Excel** from the **File** Menu.

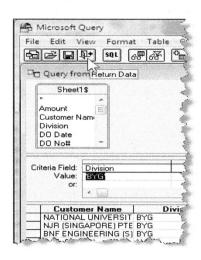

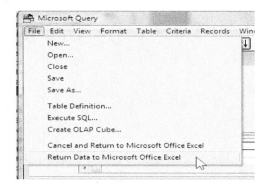

j. The pivot table now contains only data from the **BYG** division.

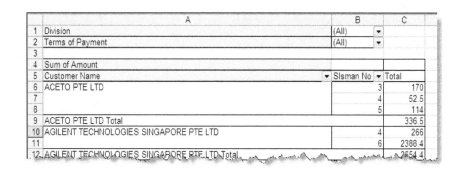

	A	B	C
1	Division	(All)	
2	Terms of Payment	(All)	
3			
4	Sum of Amount		
5	Customer Name	Slsman No	Total
6	ACETO PTE LTD	3	170
7		4	52.5
8		5	114
9	ACETO PTE LTD Total		336.5
10	AGILENT TECHNOLOGIES SINGAPORE PTE LTD	4	266
11		6	2388.4
12	AGILENT TECHNOLOGIES SINGAPORE PTE LTD Total		2654.4

End of Case 8

Case 9:   Pivot charts

Key Learning Points: Generate Pivot charts from the Pivot tables.

Case Study:

Continue from Case 7. You feel that only figures and numbers are probably not enough to present your case. You would like to create some colourful charts based on the pivot tables to further impress your boss.

Working File:

1.   *9.Pivot charts.xls*
2.   *9.Pivot charts-soln.xls*

Solution:

9.1   Generate the pivot chart

a.   Move the field **Customer Name** from the row area to the page area of the Pivot Table. Move the field **Division** to the column area.

	A	B	C	D
1				
2	Terms of Payment	(All)		
3	Customer Name	(All)		
4				
5	Sum of Amount	Division		
6	Slsman No	BYG	CCG	CYG
7	1			
8	2	191.76	536.50	
9	3	6,728.90	613.80	500.00
10	4	22,230.69	61,609.62	13,865.20
11	5	1,424.00	311.70	
12	6	103,447.97	5,603.60	34,657.35
13	7	362.80	1,801.97	
14	8	21,451.08	20,161.17	280.00
15	9	13,646.76	3,216.35	3,256.00
16	Grand Total	169,483.96	93,854.71	52,558.55
17				

b.   Move your cursor within the pivot table area; Right click and select **Pivot Chart**.

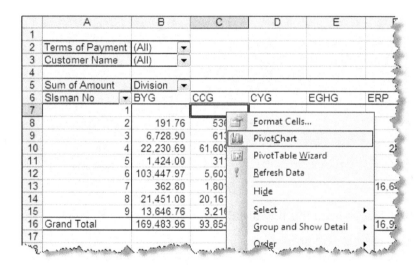

c.   The chart appears in a new sheet called **Chart 1**.

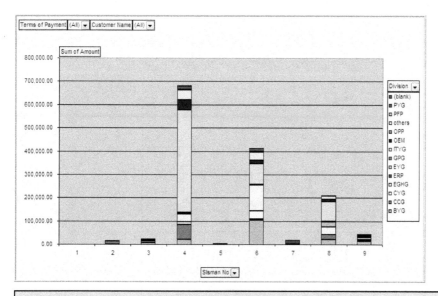

X-axis presents the values listed in the pivot table rows.

Y axis presents the values in the data area.

Each value in the column area of the pivot table is defined as a series in the chart.

9.2 Improve on the chart presentation

a. Copy the whole chart and paste it below the pivot table in the other worksheet.

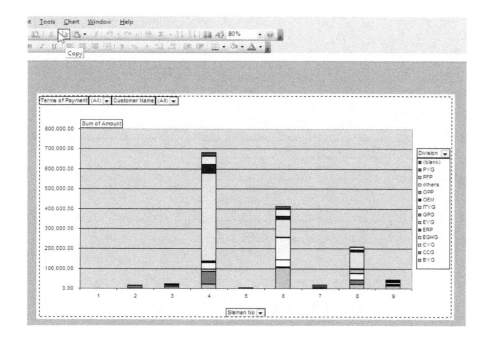

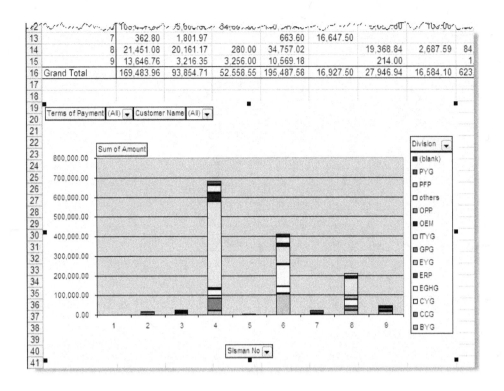

13		7	362.80	1,801.97			663.60	16,647.50			
14		8	21,451.08	20,161.17	280.00	34,757.02			19,368.84	2,687.59	84
15		9	13,646.76	3,216.35	3,256.00	10,569.18			214.00		1
16	Grand Total		169,483.96	93,854.71	52,558.55	195,487.58	16,927.50	27,946.94	16,584.10	623

b.   Move your cursor to any of the small black square, when the cursor changes to a double sided arrow, resize the chart to the preferred size.

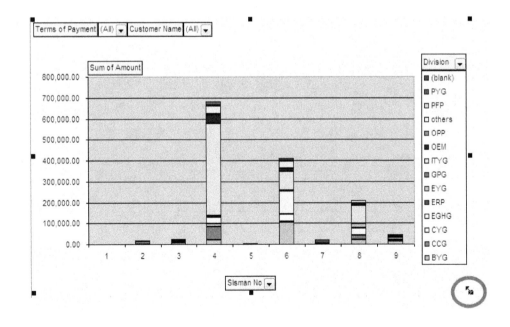

c.   Double click in the chart area, a **Format Chart Area** box pops up. Set the border and Area to **Automatic** or choose a colour of your choice for each.

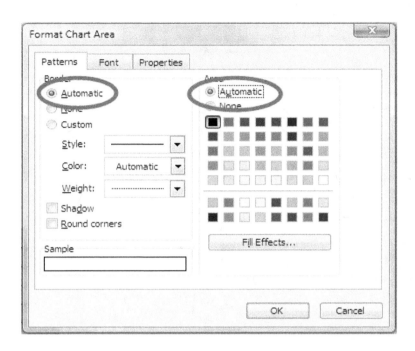

d. Go to the **Font** Tab and select the appropriate setting for the font. Make sure that you uncheck the **Auto Scale** option. This will prevent the font size from changing when the chart size changes. The setting will affect all the fonts in the charts. Click **OK**.

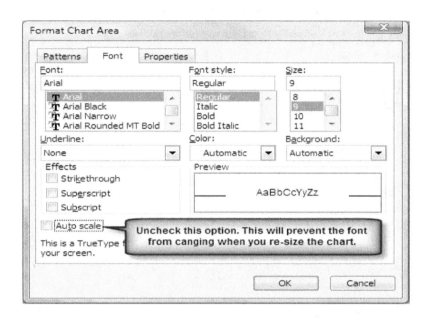

e. Move your cursor in the graph and double click.

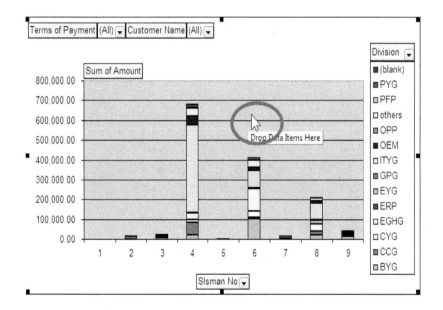

f.   Change the setting for the plot area (similar to the setting for chart area) and click **OK**.

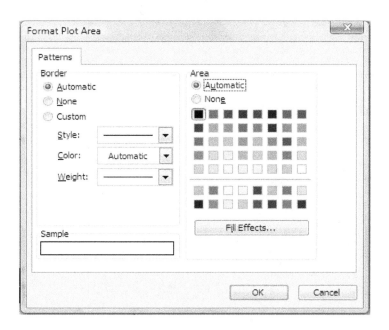

9.3   Remove the Pivot Table Fields

a.   Move your cursor to one of the fields and right click. In the popup box, click on **Hide PivotChart Field Buttons**.

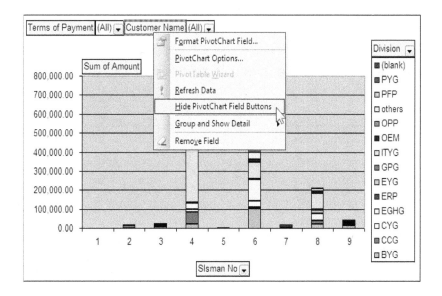

b.   The chart should look like this.

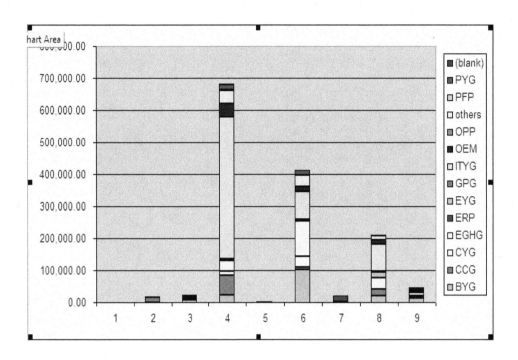

9.4   Making the field buttons re-appear in the pivot chart

a.   Look for the pivot table toolbar.

b.   If it is not there, right click on the toolbar area and select Pivot Table.

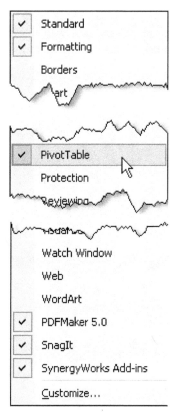

c. Select the pivot chart.

d. The label in the pivot table toolbar will change to Pivot Chart

e. Click on the Pivot Chart and check off "**Hide PivotChart Field Buttons**"

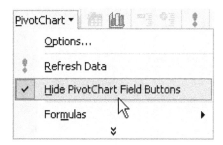

9.5 Change the Chart Type

a.   Right click in the chart area. Select the **Chart Type** option in the popup menu.

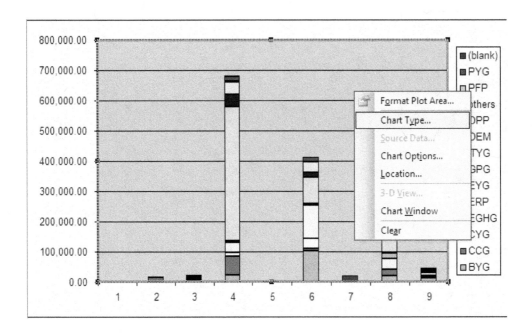

b. Select the first Option as shown.

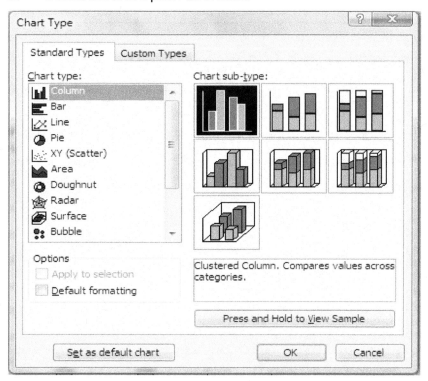

c. The chart should present the data in the following manner:

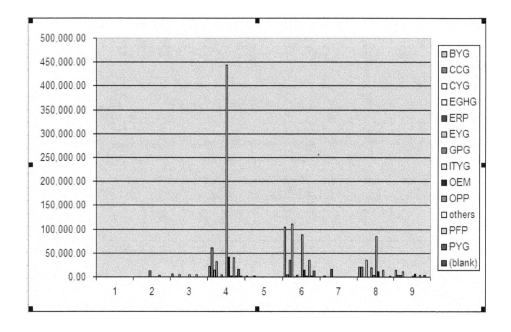

9.6 Change the x and y-axis value

The chart is controlled by the pivot table. If you change the pivot table layout, the chart will change accordingly. The x-axis is presented by the rows and the grouping within each category by the column.

a. Switch the dimensions and present the **Salesman No** in rows and the **Division** in column, the x-axis will become Divisions and within each division will show the performance of each salesman.

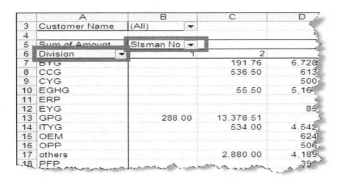

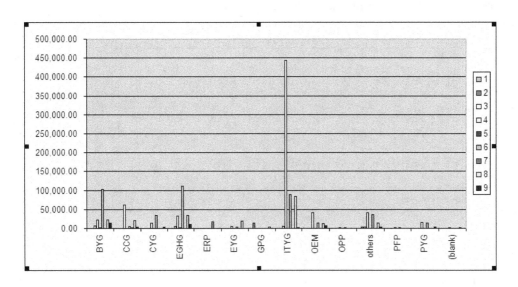

b. Right click along the x-axis or y-axis. In the popup menu, select **Format Axis**.

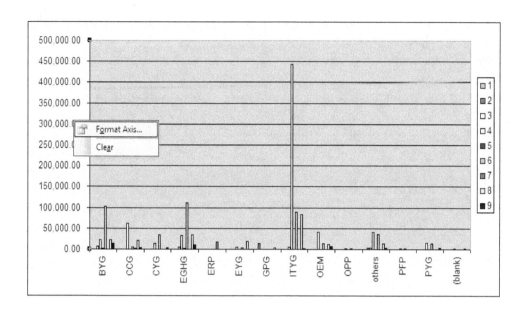

c. In the **Format Axis** box, you can format the x and y-axis as preferred.

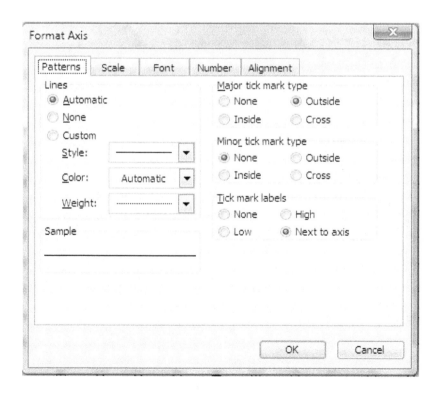

9.7 Create Multiple Pivot Charts Quickly

You can duplicate the Pivot Charts simply by duplicating the worksheets. The chart in each worksheet will be controlled by the Pivot Table within the same worksheet.

a.   Right Click at the **Sheet 1** tab and click on **Move or Copy** in the popup menu.

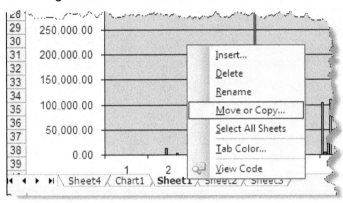

b.   Check on **Create a copy** box to duplicate this worksheet.

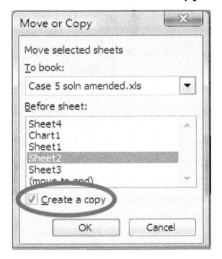

c.   When you change the layout of the pivot table in one of the worksheets, the Pivot Chart within the same worksheet will change accordingly.

End of Case 9

112

Case 10: Introduction to Macro Programming

Key Learning Points: Create a macro which formats cell or a range based on your personal preference and to activate the macro using a toolbar icon.

Case Study:

You like to present you data in your favourite colour and format, but hate to do repeat the steps in Excel whenever you have new data. Try creating a macro to assist you and save you the hassle of repeating the steps over and over again.

Solution:

10.1 Record a macro on cell formatting

a.   Open a new workbook. Enter a number in the active cell e.g. Cell B2. When you enter the number, the active cell will move to Cell B3. Make sure that you re-select Cell B2.

b. Go to Main Menu, click on **Tools → Macro → Record New Macro**

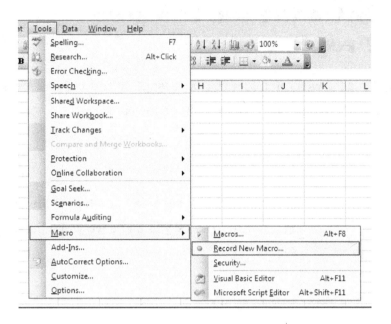

c. Enter a name for the macro e.g. **Custom_Num_Format** (note: spaces are not allowed), select to store the macro in the **Personal Macro Workbook.**

When you select to store the macro in the **Personal Macro Workbook**, the macro is saved in a hidden workbook in your computer and can be used in all workbooks. If you select **This Workbook**, macro is saved in this workbook only. It can only be used when this workbook is opened. Storing macro in the **New Workbook** is similar to **This Workbook.**

d.   Move your cursor over Cell B2, right click and select **Format Cells**.

e.   Go to the **Number** Tab. Under the category, select **Number**, check the **Use 1000 Separator (,)** box, select the negative number format with bracket and coloured red.

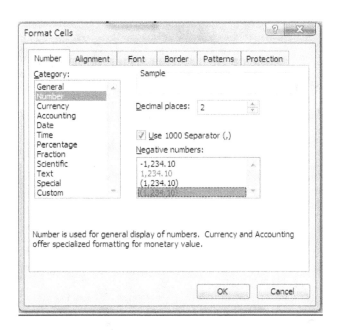

f.   Select the **Patterns** tab to format the cell with a colour of your choice and click **OK**.

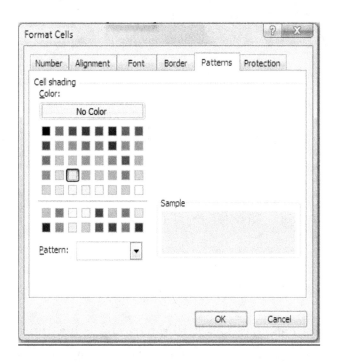

g.   Stop the Macro Recorder by clicking on the square 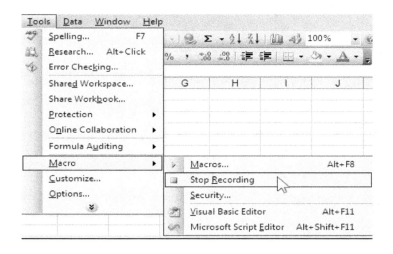 Stop Recording. Alternatively, go to Main Menu, click on **Tools → Macro → Stop Recording**.

If you are not able to see the **Stop Macro Recording** icon 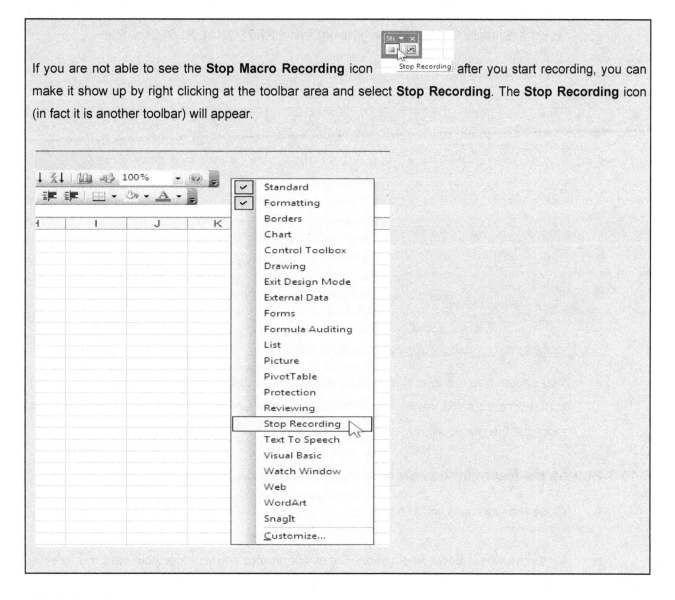 after you start recording, you can make it show up by right clicking at the toolbar area and select **Stop Recording**. The **Stop Recording** icon (in fact it is another toolbar) will appear.

10.2 Test the macro

a. Type in a number into a cell e.g. Cell F10. When you enter the number, the active cell will move to Cell F11. Make sure you re-select Cell F10 as the active cell.

b. Go to Main Menu, select **Tool → Macro → Macros**.

117

d.   Select the macro **Custom_Num_Format** in the **PERSONAL.XLS**. Click **Run**.

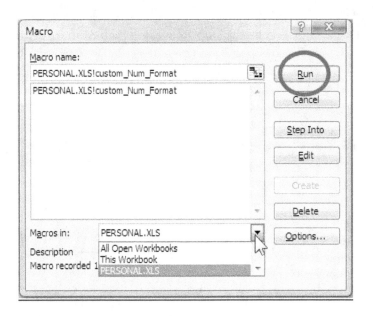

e.   You should see the format in Cell F10 changes to the format you have captured when you record your macro. If your format runs back to Cell B2, it means that you have recorded the macro slightly differently. You must re-record your macro.

10.3 Storing the Macro in the Personal Macro Workbook

a.   Close the workbook without saving.

b.   Close the whole Excel Application. Excel will prompt you whether you want to save the changes made to the personal macro workbook. Click Yes. The macro has been saved into the Personal Macro Workbook.

c.   Re-launch Excel Application and open a brand new workbook. Test the macro again to make sure that it is saved properly in the Personal Macro Workbook.

10.4 Add the Macro Icon to the Menu Bar

a.   Right click at the toolbar area. In the popup menu, select **Customize**.

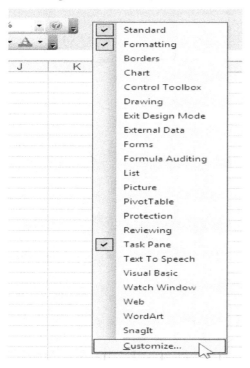

b.   Go to the **Command** Tab, select the Category called **Macros** and then select the **Custom Button** on the right.

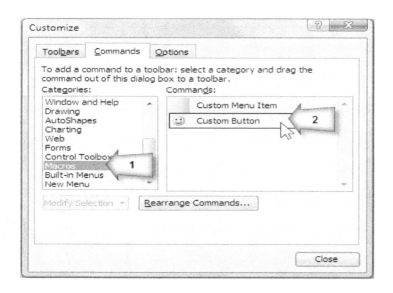

c. Click and hold the **Custom Button** icon and drag it to the Menu Bar, drop it in between other icons.

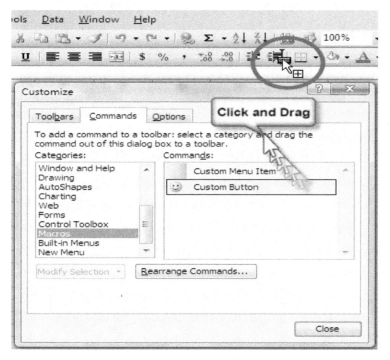

d. A happy face icon shows up. Click on **Modify Selection** and select **Assign Macro**.

120

e. Select the Macro **Custom_Num_Format** and click **OK**. This step is to link the macro to the icon. Close the dialog box.

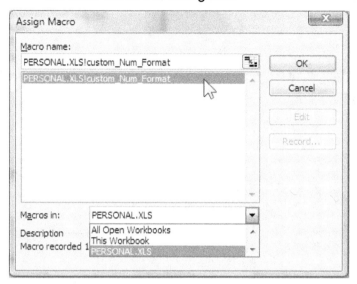

f. Go to a new cell, enter another number in the cell. Make sure that the cell is the active cell. Click on the happy face icon. You should see the format in the cell changed to your preferred format.

g. You can also change the happy face to another image. To modify the button image, right click at the toolbar area and open the **Customize** popup box.

h.   Click on the happy face icon, select **Modify Selection** and then go to **change button image**. Select your preferred image.

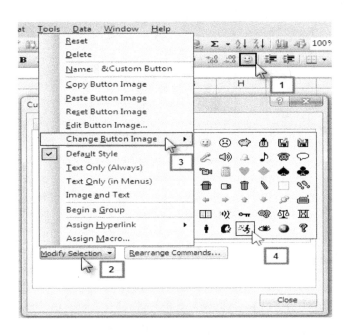

i.   Close the **Customize** popup box. The happy face icon will be changed to your preferred choice. Enter some numbers into the worksheet and test out your new icon.

j.   You can also rename the icon. In the Customize popup box, under **Modify Selection** list, go to **Name**. Replace the word **&custom button** with the name you want and hit the Enter key.

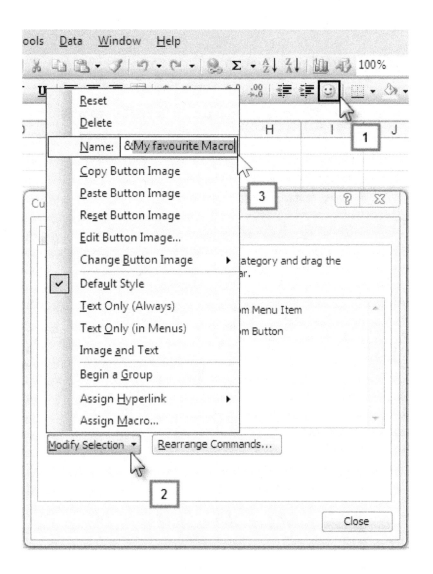

k.   When your cursor move over the icon, the description pop-up will show the name you have entered in the **Name** box.

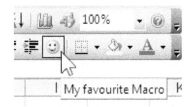

10.5 Remove the toolbar icon for the macro

a.   Right click at the toolbar area and select **Customize**.

b.   Click and drag the macro icon in the menu bar and drop it in the **Customize** dialog box.

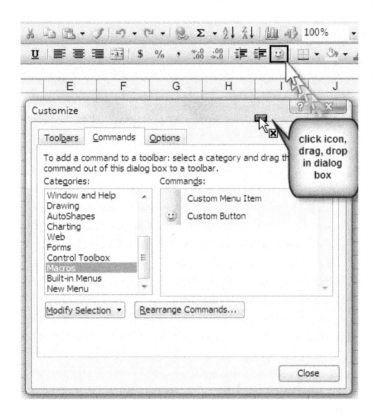

10.6 Delete the macro from the Personal Macro Workbook

a.   Go to Main Menu, click **Window → Unhide**.

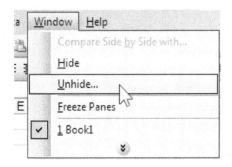

b.   Select the workbook **Personal.xls** and click **OK**.

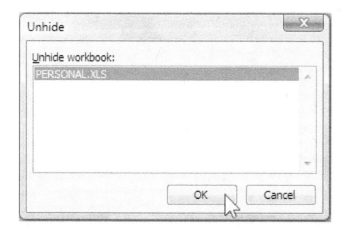

c.   Go to Main Menu and select **Tool → Macro → Macros**.

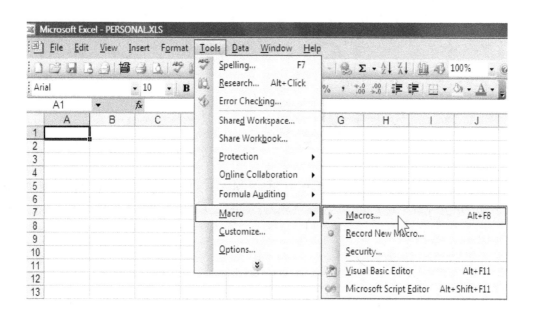

d.　Select the macro you wish to delete and click **Delete**.

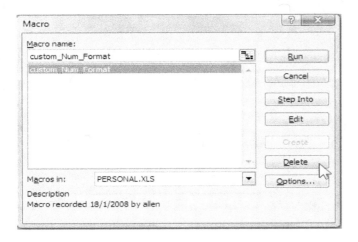

e.　When you are prompt with the message below, click **Yes**.

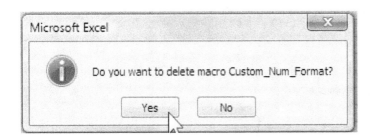

f.　To hide the **Personal Workbook**, Go to Main Menu, click **Window → Hide**. *Note: you must hide your personal workbook because it contains the settings for your new workbook.*

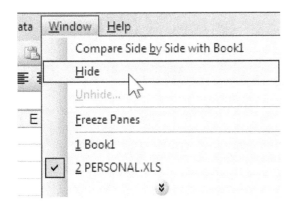

g.   Close the workbook(s) with/without saving.

h.   Close the Excel Application. Excel will prompt you whether you want to save the changes made to the personal macro workbook. Click **Yes**.

i.   The changes are saved and the macro **Custom_Num_Format** is permanently removed from the Excel Application.

End of Case 10

Case 11: Create chart that always show the most recent results

Key Learning Points: Automate the process of displaying most recent data instead of   manually updating the chart; use of the **Camera** icon.

Case Study:

Your company has recently launched a big scale promotion campaign and is expecting the sales to increase significantly during the campaign period and thereafter. You are tasked to update the sales through a chart which will show the sales for the last 14 days. You decided to create a chart that could automatically update the chart when the records is updated without losing the historical data you have.

Working File:

1.   *11.Create charts that show the most recent results.xls*
2.   *11.Create charts that show the most recent results-soln.xls*

Solution:

11.1 Create a line chart

a.   Highlight the range A25:B38.

23	22/10/2006	9616.2936
24	23/10/2006	7705.2331
25	24/10/2006	9555.3023
26	25/10/2006	6607.3899
27	26/10/2006	7847.5461
28	27/10/2006	5672.1901
29	28/10/2006	4980.9554
30	29/10/2006	4452.3643
31	30/10/2006	10490.502
32	31/10/2006	7176.6419
33	1/11/2006	10897.111
34	2/11/2006	16345.666
35	3/11/2006	4635.3381
36	4/11/2006	2805.5994
37	5/11/2006	5753.5118
38	6/11/2006	7542.5897
39	7/11/2006	10000
40		

b.   Click on the chart wizard icon 📊 on the menu bar. Select the chart type to use to present the data. You can get a preview on how your data would be presented in a particular chart type by click on the **Press and Hold to view Sample** button. This is possible because we have already defined the data range for the chart.

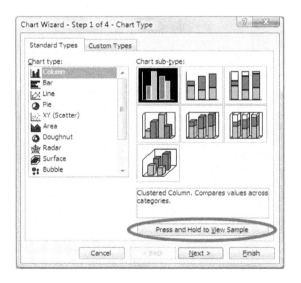

c.   In our case, we will use the line chart displayed on the top left hand corner shown in the Chart sub-Type category. Click **Next>**.

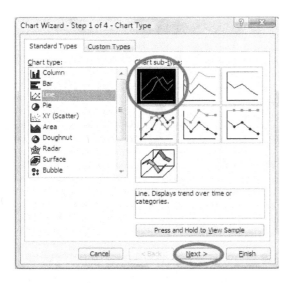

d.   In this step, no need to do anything because we have selected the data source before we start the chart wizard. Click **Next>**.

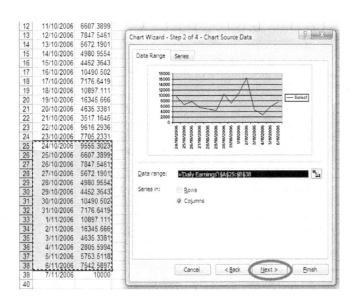

e. Fill in the title, name for your x-axis and/or y-axis here. Or you could do that later. In our case, we will do it later. Click **Next>**.

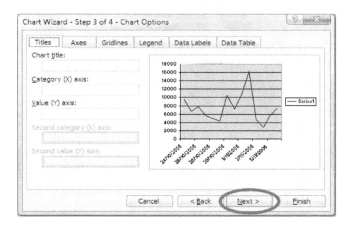

f. Place Chart as object in the **Daily Earnings** worksheet. You can do your formatting in the source data worksheet first and transfer it to another worksheet (using cut and paste chart) when you are done with the formatting.

g. This is how your chart will look like when you click **Finish**.

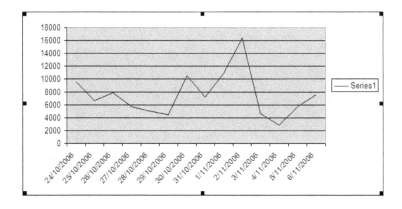

11.2 Name the chart created

a.   Right click in the Chart area and select **Source Data**.

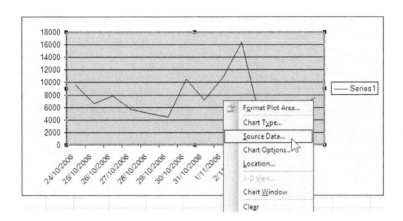

b.   Under the **series** tab, type in a name for the series in the name box. For our example, use the name **Last 14 days**.

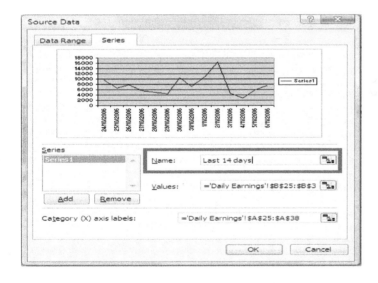

11.3 Format the chart

a. Double click anywhere outside the chart area. In the dialog box, under the **Patterns** tab, select a colour for your chart area. In the same tab, you could also format the border of the chart.

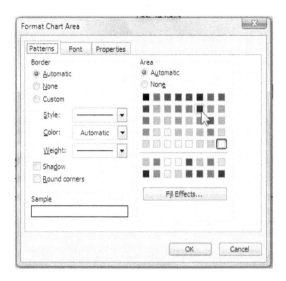

b. Go to the **Font** tab. Check off the **Auto Scale** option (found near the bottom left hand corner) so that the font size will not change automatically if you choose to re-size the chart later. Then select the preferred font format for your Chart. The font size setting is for the X axis, Y axis (name and scale) and the title. You can also set the size for these items individually.

133

c.   Then format the plot area by double clicking on the area bounded by the X and Y axes.

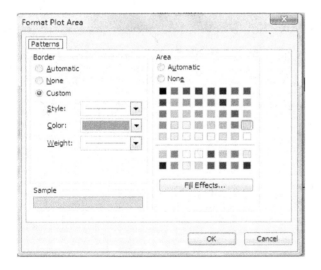

134

11.4 Present the date and the day of week on the x-axis in separate rows

The *(fx)* **TEXT** formula allows you to format a value in the desired format and convert it to a text. The formula contains 2 parts.

Part 1 - refers to the value or cell you wish to format.

Part 2 - identifies the number format you wish to display.

To find out the number format syntax, you could go to format cell, number tab and select the desired display. Then click on custom and the format for the select display will be show in the Type box.

a.   In cell C25, type in the *(fx)* **TEXT** formula **=Text(A25,"d mmm")**. The formula will return the date in A25 in the format **24 Oct**.

24	23/10/2006	7705.2331	
25	24/10/2006	9555.3023	=TEXT(A25,"d mmm")
26	25/10/2006	6607.3899	

b.   To display the day of the week, type the symbol "**&**" after the 1st formula followed by the *(fx)* **TEXT** formula **=Text(A25,"ddd")**.

24	23/10/2006	7705.2331	
25	24/10/2006	9555.3023	=TEXT(A25,"d mmm")&TEXT(A25,"ddd")
26	25/10/2006	6607.3899	

c.   To break the 2 set of information into 2 rows, add in a *(fx)* **CHAR** formula between them, joined by another "**&**". The char(13) is the code for line break. The formula will become **=Text(A25,"d mmm")&Char(13)&Text(A25,"ddd").** Copy the formula down to the last row (C38).

24	23/10/2006	7705.2331	
25	24/10/2006	9555.3023	=TEXT(A25,"d mmm")&CHAR(13)&TEXT(A25,"ddd")
26	25/10/2006	6607.3899	

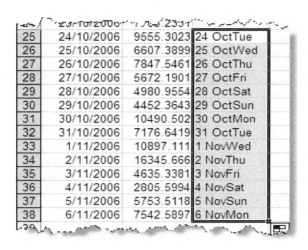

25	24/10/2006	9555.3023	24 OctTue
26	25/10/2006	6607.3899	25 OctWed
27	26/10/2006	7847.5461	26 OctThu
28	27/10/2006	5672.1901	27 OctFri
29	28/10/2006	4980.9554	28 OctSat
30	29/10/2006	4452.3643	29 OctSun
31	30/10/2006	10490.502	30 OctMon
32	31/10/2006	7176.6419	31 OctTue
33	1/11/2006	10897.111	1 NovWed
34	2/11/2006	16345.666	2 NovThu
35	3/11/2006	4635.3381	3 NovFri
36	4/11/2006	2805.5994	4 NovSat
37	5/11/2006	5753.5118	5 NovSun
38	6/11/2006	7542.5897	6 NovMon

d.   Outside the chart area, right click and select **Source Data**.

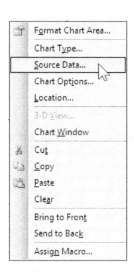

e.   Under the **Series** tab, in the **Category (X) axis labels**, change the range from $A$25:$A$38 to $C$25:$C$38. Click **OK**.

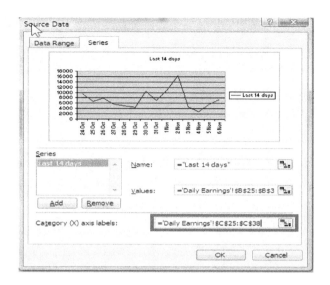

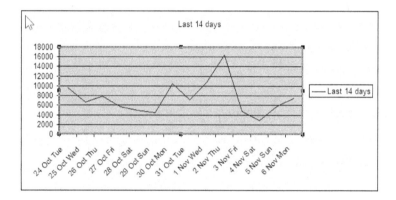

f.   To make the chart display the description in 2 lines, you have to align the x-axis label. Move your mouse slightly below the x axis and right click. Select **format axis**. Alternatively, you can double click slightly below the x-axis line.

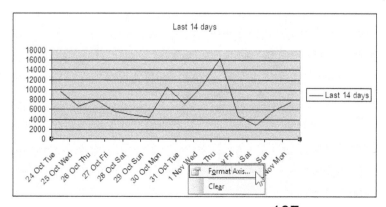

137

g.   Under the **Alignment** tab, click on the red diamond. This will set the **Automatic** option off.

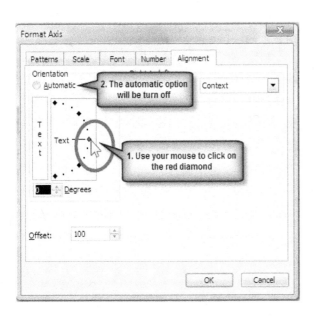

h.   Click **OK** and the x-axis description will be displayed in 2 lines.

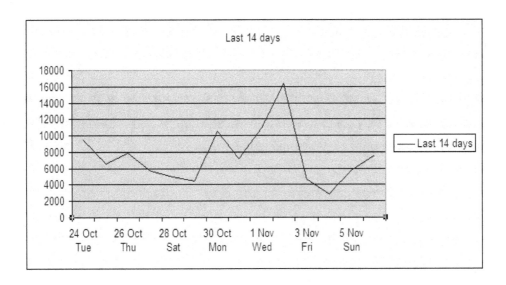

11.5 Display the description for Sundays only

The (𝑓x) **WEEKDAY** formula consists of 2 parts:

Part 1: The date which you would like to find the day of week.

Part 2: The (𝑓x) **WEEKDAY** formula will return a number (1 to 7) representing the day of the week. To cater to different countries' preference, Excel has provided 3 options:

    1 is the default setting. It will return Sunday as 1, Monday as 2... Saturday as 7.

    2 will return Monday as 1, Tuesday as 2,.. and Sunday as 7.

    3 will return Monday as 0, Tuesday as 2,...Sunday as 6.

a.   Using the (𝑓x) **WEEKDAY** formula, we can identify the day of the week for a date. In our example, we will only show the dates for 2 Sundays in the last 14 days.

b.   By setting the (𝑓x) **WEEKDAY** formula **Weekday(A2,2)=7** as the condition in the (𝑓x) **If** formula, we can check if a particular date falls on a Sun. If it does, return the day number and description i.e. **Text(A25,"d mmm")&Char(13)&Text(A25,"ddd").** If it is not, return a blank. The full formula is

=If(Weekday(A25,2)=7, Text(A25,"d mmm")&Char(13)&Text(A25,"ddd"),"")

c.   Put the above formula in cell C25 and copy down to cell C38. The results should be as follows :

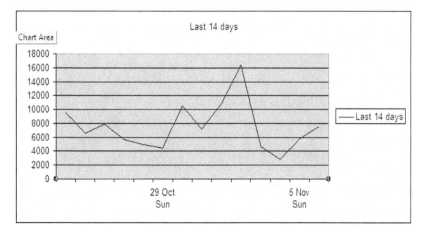

d. If you don't see the presentation as shown, double click over the x-axis. Under the **Scale** tab, make sure that the **Number of categories between tick mark labels** is set to **1**.

11.6 Remove the series label

a. Click at the Series label and press [Del] Key.

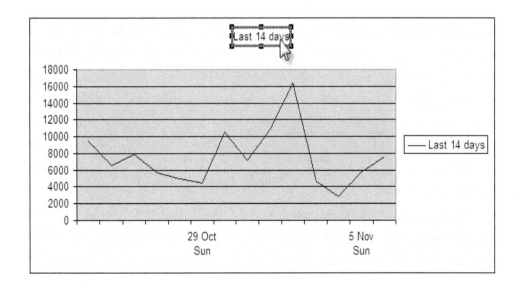

11.7 Make the chart shows only the last 14 days results automatically

The (fx) **OFFSET** formula returns a cell or range reference using another cell as a benchmark. It works like a relative cell referencing.

e.g. =Offset(A1,0,0,1,1)

Using this (fx) **OFFSET** formula for explanation,

Cell **A1**, **=Offset(A1,0,0,1,1)** is the starting point.

The two **0**s, **=Offset(A1,0,0,1,1)** indicates that the target cell reference is zero row and zero column from cell A1. This means that the target cell reference begins in cell A1.

The two **1**s, **=Offset(A1,0,0,1,1)** indicates that the reference is ONE row high and ONE column wide i.e. one cell. This means that the entire (fx) **OFFSET** formula **=Offset(A1,0,0,1,1)** refers to cell A1. If we change two 1s into two 2s, the target reference would become **=A1:B2**. In the illustration below, the target reference would be A1:B4.

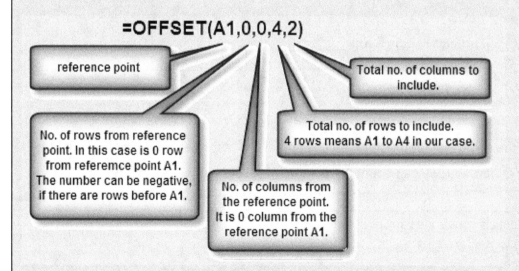

To test the formula, press the function [F5] key (Goto function) and enter the entire formula including the equal sign ("=") into the reference area. Click OK. Excel will highlight the range A1:B4.

a. To make the graph range dynamic so that it will always show the trend for the last 14 days, we can use the **(fx) OFFSET** formula together with the name range.

b. First set up a basic **(fx) OFFSET** formula in an empty cell (e.g. D2) to read the first cell (A1) in the worksheet. The formula is **=Offset($A$1,0,0,1,1)**. The formula returns the cell reference A1 and thus show the value in A1. It is similar to typing in the formula **=A1** into the cell F2.

	A	B	C	D	E
1	Date	Earnings	New X-axis		
2	1/10/2006	9412.9893		=offset($A$1,0,0,1,1)	
3	2/10/2006	9169.0241			

c. To read the cell in C1, we need to change the 2nd zero in the **(fx) OFFSET** formula to 2. (The **(fx) OFFSET** formula starts the count from zero, i.e. Column A is zero. Therefore, column C is 2.) The **(fx) OFFSET** formula becomes **=Offset($A$1,0,2,1,1)**.

	A	B	C	D	E	F	G	H
1	Date	Earnings	New X-axis					
2	1/10/2006	9412.9893		=offset($A$1,0,2,1,1)				
3	2/10/2006	9169.0241			OFFSET(reference, rows, **cols**, [height], [width])			

d. As for the rows, we need to find the position of the last row in the range. Using the **(fx) COUNTA** formula, we can count the number of records in the column B.

The **(fx) COUNTA** formula counts the number of **non-blank cells** within a range.

To count the number of rows to include, we can use =**Counta($B:$B)**.

To count the number of columns, we can use the following formula =**Counta($1:$1)**.

*Note: Users are not allowed to enter any workings within this range. It will be included in the **(fx) COUNTA** formula and return the wrong range.*

142

e. To refer to the last row in column B in the (*fx*) *OFFSET* formula, we need to deduct 1 from the (*fx*) *COUNTA* formula. This is because the (*fx*) *OFFSET* formula start counting from zero but the (*fx*) *COUNTA* formula starts from 1. Therefore, the position of the last row in column is **=Counta($B:$B)-1**.

f. Since our x-axis range for the graph starts 13 rows from the last row (last 14 days), we need to minus another 13 units from the (*fx*) *COUNTA* formula. Therefore the (*fx*) *COUNTA* formula becomes **=Counta($B:$B)-1-13** OR **=Counta($B:$B)-14**. Replace the first **1** in the (*fx*) *OFFSET* formula with this new formula which is

=offset($A$1, Counta($B:$B)-14, 2,1,1).

	A	B	C	D	E	F	G	H
1	Date	Earnings	New X-axis					
2	1/10/2006	9412.9893		=OFFSET($A$1, COUNTA($B:$B)-14, 2,1,1)				
3	2/10/2006	9169.0241						
4	3/10/2006	18460.031						
5	4/10/2006	12299.91						
	5/10/2006	13963.896						

g. To return a range, increase the number in the last 2 parts of the (*fx*) *OFFSET* formula. To return a range that contains 14 rows (14 days of data), increase the 1 in the last 2nd part to 14. Since we are dealing with only 1 column, we will keep the 1 in the last part of the offset formula. This will be the formula for X-axis

=Offset($A$1,Counta($B:$B)-14, 2,14,1).

h. Note: the formula in Cell D2 will return **#VALUE!** because Excel cannot return the result of a range in a cell. You can check whether you have set up the correct formula by using the **Go To** function (F5 key).

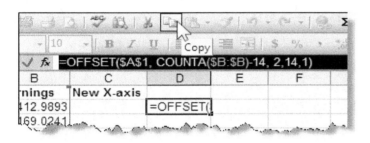

	A	B	C	D	E	F
1	Date	Earnings	New X-axis			
2	1/10/2006	9412.9893	◇	#VALUE!		
3	2/10/2006	9169.0241				
4	3/10/2006	10160.031				

fx =OFFSET($A$1, COUNTA($B:$B)-14, 2,14,1)

i. Highlight and copy the entire **(fx) OFFSET** formula **=Offset($A$1,Counta($B:$B)-14, 2,14,1)**. Press the [Esc] key.

=OFFSET($A$1, COUNTA($B:$B)-14, 2,14,1)

B	C	D	E	F
nings	New X-axis			
12.9893		=OFFSET(		
69.0241				

j. Press [F5] key to activate the **Go To** function. Paste the formula into the reference text box and click OK. (Note : use [Ctrl] key + letter [V] key to paste only.)

Go To

Go to:
$D$2

Reference:
=OFFSET($A$1, COUNTA($B:$B)-14, 2,14,1)

Special...   OK   Cancel

k. If the formula is working properly, it will highlight the range in the worksheet.

24	23/10/2006	7705.2331	
25	24/10/2006	9555.3023	
26	25/10/2006	6607.3899	
27	26/10/2006	7847.5461	
28	27/10/2006	5672.1901	
29	28/10/2006	4980.9554	
30	29/10/2006	4452.3643	29 OctSun
31	30/10/2006	10490.502	
32	31/10/2006	7176.6419	
33	1/11/2006	10897.111	
34	2/11/2006	16345.666	
35	3/11/2006	4635.3381	
36	4/11/2006	2805.5994	
37	5/11/2006	5753.5118	5 NovSun
38	6/11/2006	7542.5897	
39			

l.   Create a similar formula for the y-axis in cell E3. The formula for Y-axis will be **=Offset($A$1,Counta($B:$B)-14, 1,14,1)**. Check the formula with the goto special function to make sure that it is valid.

m.   If the formula is working properly, it will highlight the range in the worksheet.

24	23/10/2006	7705.2331	
25	24/10/2006	9555.3023	
26	25/10/2006	6607.3899	
27	26/10/2006	7847.5461	
28	27/10/2006	5672.1901	
29	28/10/2006	4980.9554	
30	29/10/2006	4452.3643	29 OctSun
31	30/10/2006	10490.502	
32	31/10/2006	7176.6419	
33	1/11/2006	10897.111	
34	2/11/2006	16345.666	
35	3/11/2006	4635.3381	
36	4/11/2006	2805.5994	
37	5/11/2006	5753.5118	5 NovSun
38	6/11/2006	7542.5897	
39			

11.8 Create names for the x-axis and y-axis

Why do we have to create a name for the x-axis and y-axis?

In Excel charts, we are required to enter a range reference each for the x-axis and y-axis. The chart can only accept a static range e.g. A1:Z100 or a range name but not a formula. Since our range is a dynamic range and range name can accept dynamic range, we can use it for the x-axis and y-axis.

a. Highlight and copy the formula in cell D2. Then hit the Esc key to keep the formula in cell D2.

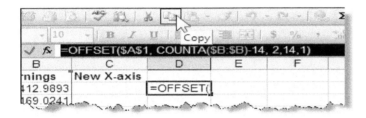

b. Go to Main Menu, select **Insert → Name → Define**.

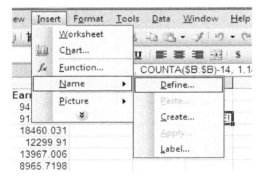

c. Enter a meaningful name for the range. In this example, let's use the name "**x_axis_range**". Paste (press Ctrl key + letter V key together) the formula into the **Refers to** box.

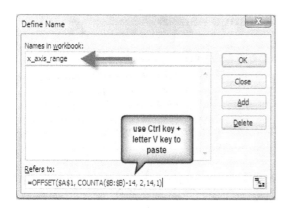

d. Click on the **Add** button to put the range name in the list. Repeat the steps above for the y-axis range. (The formula is in Cell E3.)

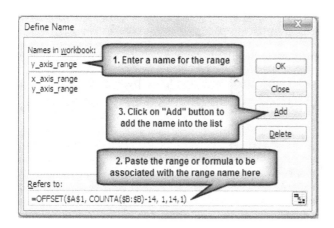

e. When you have added all the range names, close the dialog box by clicking on the **Close** button.

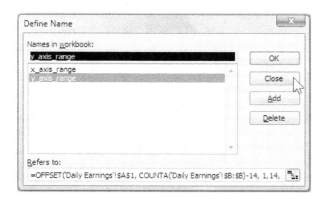

Note: All the ranges must be locked (i.e. using absolute reference). If they are not locked, the ranges are likely to deviate from our designated cell(s) reference. This is because range name still obey the relative reference rule.

147

11.9 Replace the x-axis and y-axis ranges with range names

a. Right click over the chart area and select **Source Data**.

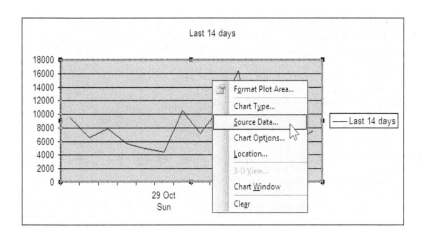

b. Enter the name of the y-axis range into the **Values** box. The workbook name must precede the range name. In our case, the text to enter into the value box is **='Last 14 Days Earnings.xls'!y_axis_range** (include the single quotation marks for the workbook name)

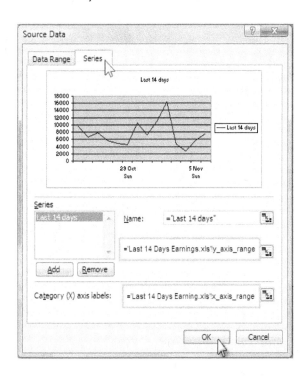

c. Your chart will now show the earnings per day for the last 14 days. When new records are added, the chart will reflect the new record and the previous 13 days of earnings.

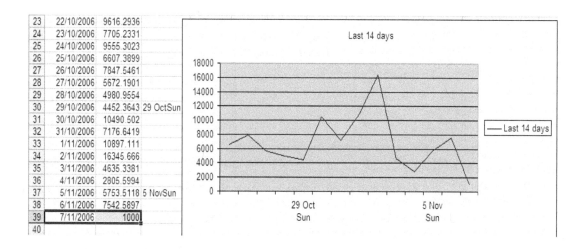

23	22/10/2006	9616.2936	
24	23/10/2006	7705.2331	
25	24/10/2006	9555.3023	
26	25/10/2006	6607.3899	
27	26/10/2006	7847.5461	
28	27/10/2006	5672.1901	
29	28/10/2006	4980.9554	
30	29/10/2006	4452.3643	29 OctSun
31	30/10/2006	10490.502	
32	31/10/2006	7176.6419	
33	1/11/2006	10897.111	
34	2/11/2006	16345.666	
35	3/11/2006	4635.3381	
36	4/11/2006	2805.5994	
37	5/11/2006	5753.5118	5 NovSun
38	6/11/2006	7542.5897	
39	7/11/2006	1000	
40			

11.10 Making the chart change colour based on performance

a. Double click on the chart area. The safest area should be the area above the trend line. Remove the chart area colour by selecting **None**. Click **OK**.

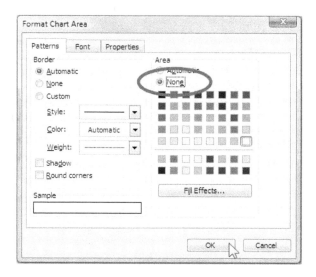

149

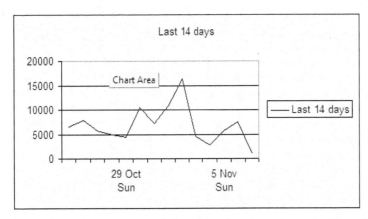

b.   Insert a new worksheet and cut and paste the chart to cell B2 of the new worksheet. Enlarge cell B2 and adjust the chart such that the chart fits nicely into the cell.

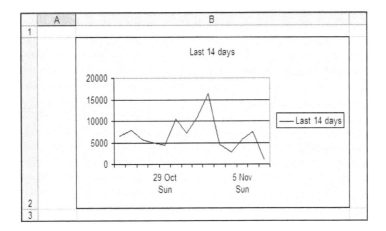

When you are moving or adjusting the chart with the mouse, you can press and hold on to the `Alt` key to make the chart edges snap to the grid lines.

c.   Set up conditional formatting in Cell B2 for the following conditions (note: you need to move behind the chart. Try to select Cell B1 and use the `↓` key to move down to B2)

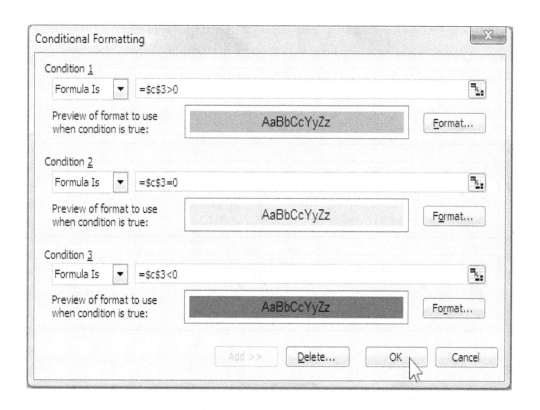

d.	Test the setting by entering 1, 0 and -1 into the cell C3 one by one to make sure cell B2 change to the appropriate colour.

e.	Enter the formula in cell C3 to check the last day value is against the last second day value. We can reuse the (*f*x) **OFFSET** formula by changing our y-axis (*f*x) **OFFSET** formula. Instead of 14 days, change it to 1 to identify only one cell

=Offset('Daily Earnings'!$A$1, Counta('Daily Earnings'!$B:$B)-1,1,1,1)

f.	Then re-use the offset formula to subtract the last second day value from the last day value.

=Offset('Daily Earnings'!$A$1, Counta('Daily Earnings'!$B:$B)-2, 1,1,1)

g.	The final formula in Cell C3 should be

=Offset('Daily Earnings'!$A$1, Counta('Daily Earnings'!$B:$B)-1,1,1,1)- Offset('Daily Earnings'!$A$1, Counta('Daily Earnings'!$B:$B)-2, 1,1,1)

151

h.   Now, when the last day earnings is less than last second day, the chart will turn red, if it is the same, it will turn peach and if is more, it will turn green.

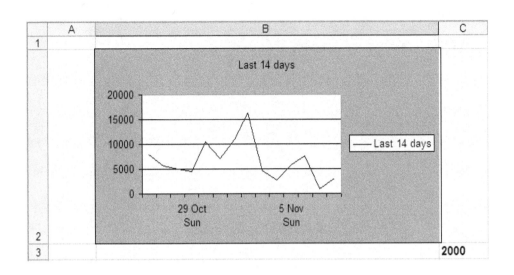

11.11 Activate the Camera in Customize box -> Tool.

a.   The Camera icon is not available in the menu bar. It is activated only through the use of customised menu. Right click in the visible toolbars area and select **Customize**.

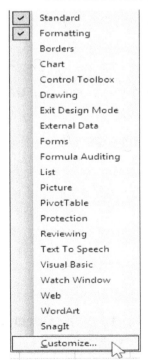

b. Under the **Commands** tab, Select **Tools** Category and find the **Camera** button as shown, drag and drop it in the menu bar.

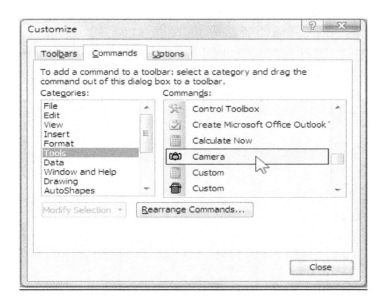

c. Highlight a range you want to view (named the first range). In this example, highlight the range of **A1:B20** of the **Daily Earnings** worksheet.

	A	B	
1	Date	Earnings	New
2	1/10/2006	9412.9893	
3	2/10/2006	9169.0241	
4	3/10/2006	18460.031	
5	4/10/2006	12299.91	
6	5/10/2006	13967.006	
7	6/10/2006	8965.7198	
8	7/10/2006	3517.1645	
9	8/10/2006	9616.2936	
10	9/10/2006	7705.2331	
11	10/10/2006	9555.3023	
12	11/10/2006	6607.3899	
13	12/10/2006	7847.5461	
14	13/10/2006	5672.1901	
15	14/10/2006	4980.9554	
16	15/10/2006	4452.3643	
17	16/10/2006	10490.502	
18	17/10/2006	7176.6419	
19	18/10/2006	10897.111	
20	19/10/2006	16345.666	
21	20/10/2006	4635.3381	

153

d. Click on the 📷 camera icon. Go to sheet1, place your cursor at the cell below the chart and click. The highlighted range appeared on the worksheet like a picture. (Named the second range). You can now view changes in the first range using the second range.

11.12 Adjust the size of the picture

a. Click on the picture to have it selected, move the mouse to the bottom right hand corner of picture to adjust the size of the picture.

12/10/2006	7847.5461
13/10/2006	5672.1901
14/10/2006	4980.9554
15/10/2006	4452.3643
16/10/2006	10490.502
17/10/2006	7176.6419
18/10/2006	10897.111
19/10/2006	16345.666

End of Case 11

Case 12: Create a Form in Excel

Key Learning Points: Create Forms.

Case Study:

You are imparting computer skills as a living. You would like to improve your teaching skills, therefore, the feedbacks from the participants are important. You want to create a useful form/questionnaire that allows you to collect and consolidate the data in seconds without needing another person to re-enter the data into the database.

Working File:

1. *12. Create a Form in Excel.xls*
2. *12. Create a Form in Excel-soln.xls*

Solution:

12.1 Create a Dropdown list using Data Validation

a.   Select Cell B6 in the worksheet. Go to Main Menu, select **Data → Validation**.

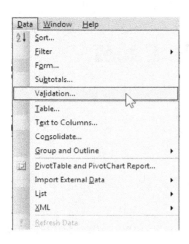

b. In the Data Validation dialog box, select the **Settings** tab. In the **Validation** criteria, Under **Allow:** section, choose **List**. Under the **Source:** section, enter the range name **=Title** as it is in another worksheet (Sheet2). The name range **Title** has been preset in Sheet2. (refer to case 19 on how to create a range name) .

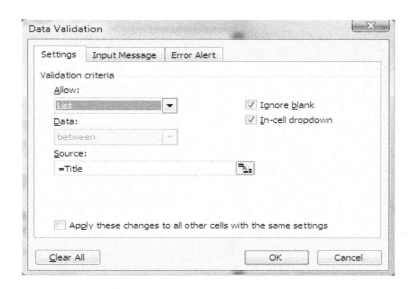

c. If the range is in the same worksheet as the form, you can replace the named range with a normal range e.g. A1:A10.

d. When click on the dropdown arrow button on the right side, the list is shown for selection.

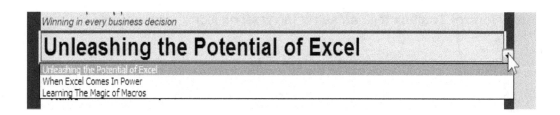

e. In Sheet2 Cell A2, create a link to Sheet1 cell B6. This is to capture the title selected by the participants.

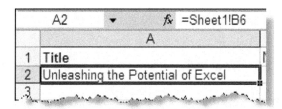

12.2 Create a Textbox from control toolbox

a. Right click at the **Toolbar** area and activate the toolbar called **Control Toolbox**.

b.   In the **Control Toolbox** toolbar, select the **textbox** icon.

c.   At the blank space next to **Name**: (Cell E8) draw the textbox to the size you want. To align the text box to the cell border, press and hold the [Alt] key as you re-size the textbox with your mouse.

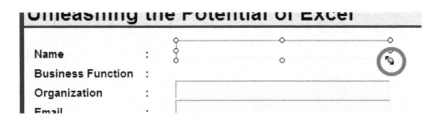

d.   Make sure that the control toolbar is on design mode, the icon appears depressed.

e. Right click in the text box and select **Properties**.

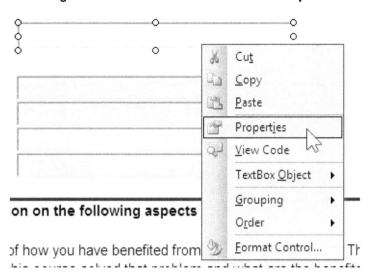

f. In the **LinkedCell** area, type in **Sheet2!B2**. This is to capture the answer in Sheet2 Cell B2 of the workbook.

12.3 Create a Dropdown Box (labelled as Combo Box) from control toolbox

a. A dropdown box will allow you to select the answer from a list or to enter an answer that is not found in the list. In the **Control Toolbox** toolbar, select the **Combo Box** icon.

b. At Cell E9, draw the combo box to the size you want. To align the combo box to the cell border, press and hold the Alt key while re-sizing.

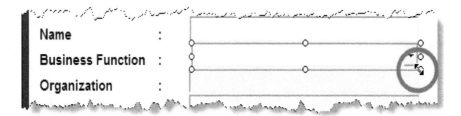

c. Make sure that the control toolbar is on design mode, the icon appears depressed.

d.   Right click in the combo box and select **Properties**.

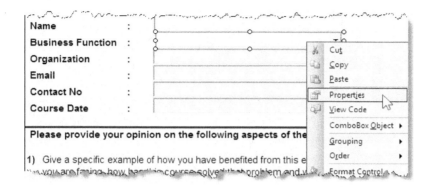

e.   In the **LinkedCell** area, type in **Sheet2!C2**. This is to capture the answer in Sheet2 Cell C2 of the workbook.

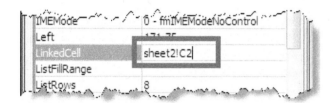

f.   In the **ListFillRange** which is just below the **LinkedCell**, type in the range for the list, i.e. **Sheet2!C11:C17**. This will pick up the list of business functions typed in cell C11 to C17.

g.   This is the range of values that will be presented in the combo box.

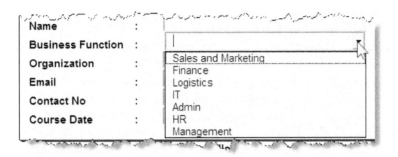

12.4 Create an Option Button

a.   An Option Button only allows the user to select one answer for the question. In the **Control Toolbox** toolbar, select the **Option Button** icon.

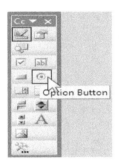

b.   At the right side of Question 5, draw the **Option** button to the size you want. To align the **Option** button to the cell border, press and hold the [Alt] key while re-sizing.

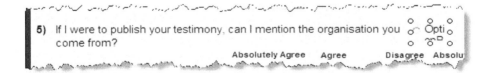

c.   Copy and paste another **Option** button. One of them would be a **Yes** and the other a **No**.

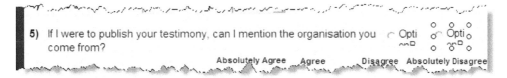

d.   Make sure that the control toolbar is on design mode, the icon appears depressed.

e.   Right click at one of the Option Buttons. From the pop up menu, select **OptionButton Object → Edit**.

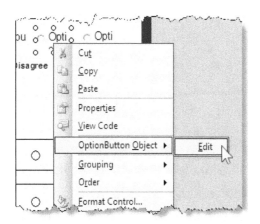

163

f. Type in the text **Yes** into the label for one of the Option Buttons. Right click at the other Option Button and type in the text **No**.

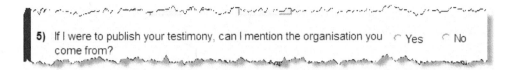

5) If I were to publish your testimony, can I mention the organisation you come from?   ○ Yes   ○ No

g. Right click again at one of the Option Buttons and select **Properties**.

h. In the **LinkedCell** area, type in **Sheet2!L2**. This is to capture the answer in Sheet2 Cell L2 of the workbook.

i. If you have more than one set of option buttons, you need to group each set together so that each set will work independently from the other set. To group them together. In the second set of option buttons, right click on one of the buttons and select **Properties**. In the **GroupName**, change to any other name to differentiate it from the first group. Repeat for the other option button in the second set.

164

12.5 Create a Range of Scale

a. A range of scale is a series of option buttons where users can choose only one number from the scale. It works like the Yes and No option button except that the scale has more than 2 option buttons most of the time. To create a range of scale and capture the score, the option button in the **Forms** menu is recommended.

b. Right click at the **Toolbar** area and activate the toolbar called **Forms**.

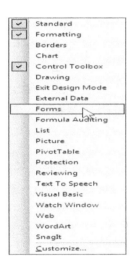

c. Click on the **Option button** icon in the **Forms** toolbar.

d. At question 6, draw the **Option Button** to the size you want.

e. Right click and select **Edit Text**.

f. Replace the option button text with the relevant description (In our case, we are not putting in any text).

g. Right click on the **Option** Button and select copy. Select a cell and click **Paste** to create a copy of the option button. In this way, you will have option buttons of the same size.

h.   Right click at one of the Option Buttons and select **Format Control** which is listed as the last item in the menu.

i.   Under the **Control** tab, in the textbox for **Cell link**, input the cell M2 of sheet2 where you want to capture the answer. Click **OK**. Note that the rest of the buttons are also linked to cell M2 of sheet2.

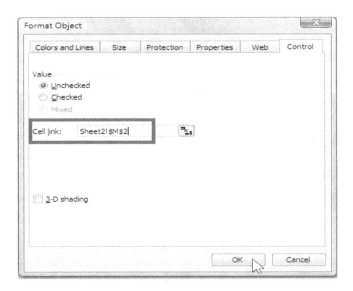

167

12.6 If you have more than 1 set of radio buttons

a.   Click on the **Group Box** icon.

b.   Draw the group box to include all the buttons that belongs to question 6. This set of option buttons will work independently with other groups.

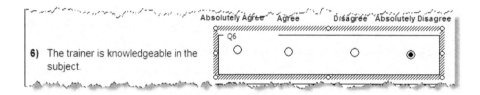

12.7 Create a Checkbox from control toolbox

a.   Click on the **Check Box** icon.

b.   At Question 10, draw the checkbox to the appropriate size.

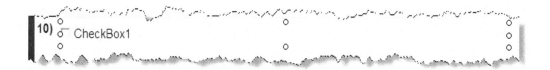

c.   Right click and select **CheckBox Object → Edit**.

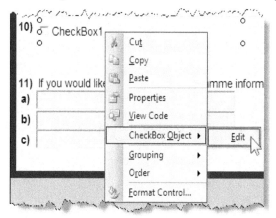

d.   Replace the checkbox text with "**I am interested to learn more about the course: When Excel Comes In Power**".

e.   Right click and select **Copy**. Select a cell and click **Paste** to create a copy of the check box. In this way, you will have check boxes of the same size. Change the text to "**I am interested to learn more about the course: Learning the magic of macros**".

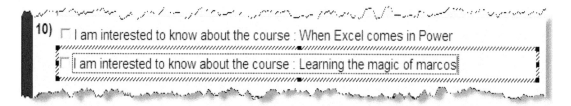

f.   Right click at the first check box area and select **Properties**.

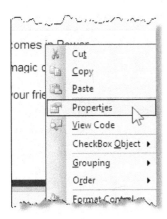

g.   In the **LinkedCell** area, type in **Sheet2!Q2**. This is to capture the answer in Sheet2 Cell Q2 of the workbook. Close the **properties** box.

h.   Link the other check box to **Sheet2!R2**. Each check box has its own answer of TRUE or FALSE. Therefore, each checkbox should have a cell to capture the answer.

12.8 Launch the Form

a.   Once you have completed designing the entire form, you can activate the form by exiting out of its design mode (see picture below). Save the worksheet and your form is ready for use.

12.9 Capture the answers

a.   If you have arranged the answers to the questions in one single row, according to the sequence of questions, in sheet2, you can easily copy the entire row of answers for each completed form to your consolidation worksheet for analysis.

End of Case 12

Case 13: Consolidate data from different workbooks

Key Learning Points: Manage multiple data sources with MS Query; create dynamic range for pivot tables, (*f*x) **OFFSET** formula, (*f*x) **COUNTA** formula.

Case Study:

You are in the regional HQ. And you are tasked to consolidate the monthly sales figures from the countries in the region and prepare consolidated reports on a monthly basis. Besides monthly sales reports, you are also asked to present YTD figures for each company and consolidated sales and YTD sales reports for all companies.

Working File:

13. Consolidate data from diff workbooks.xls
13. Consolidate data from diff workbooks-soln.xls
13. Consolidate data from diff workbooks-backup.xls

Solution:

In real situation, this solution will help you obtain auto updates on the 3 files managed by 3 different people. To make sure that it works well, you must prepare the following:

1. Make sure that the 3 files have the same common fields so that you do not get yourself confused with the numbers.

2. You must install MS Query function into your computer/laptop. This function comes free when you purchase MSOffice. But it is not included in the standard installation.

About MS Query

MS Query is a simple but powerful ad-hoc query tool that you can use to retrieve and organize data from databases (such as Access, SQL database server, Dbase, or even Excel worksheets, just to name a few). The retrieved data can be displayed directly on a MS Excel worksheet for further editing or be presented in a pivot table, pivot chart report or just as list of records.

The feature is readily available in MSOffice but not installed in the standard setup. To check whether this function is installed in your computer, please refer to Appendix 1.

13.1 Create the first data source

Note: We have put the 3 files into 1 workbook for ease of use.

a. Open a brand new workbook. In the worksheet sheet1, select **Data → Import External Data → New Database Query** under the Main Menu.

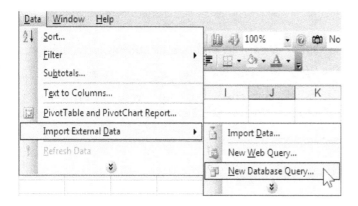

b.   Select **Excel Files** as the data source, uncheck the option **Use the Query Wizard to create/edit queries** and click **OK**.

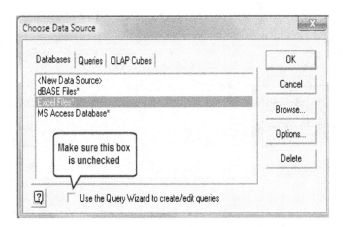

In our example, we select Excel files as the data. You can use the same method to access dBase Files, MS Access and for some of you SQL databases (SQL database are database servers which is used to stored huge amount of records, most probably in the millions.

Also, please make sure that the option **Use the Query Wizard to create/edit queries** is unchecked. This is more of my personal preference. I find that it is easier to work with the query on my own than to use the wizard. After you have learnt my method, you can always come back to try out how the wizard works.

c.   In the next dialog box **Select Workbook**, choose the file you want to work with. For our case, the name is **Consolidate data from diff workbooks.xls** and click **OK**.

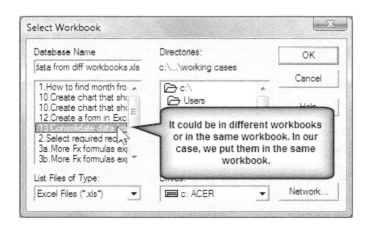

d.   In the **Add Tables** box, select the first file **SG$** and click **Add** before closing the dialog box.

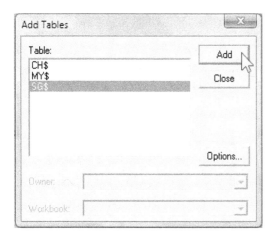

e.   Double Click on the * sign to present all the fields.

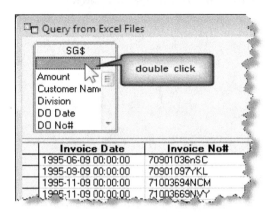

13.2 Remove duplicate records from the database

a.   Browse to the last account and you should see 645 records.

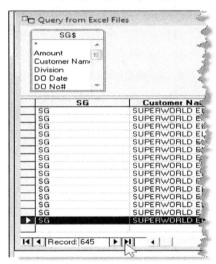

b.   In the database, there are a total of 9 duplicate records. To remove them, go to the **Menu**, select **View → Query Properties**.

c. Check the box for **Unique Values Only**.

d. If you browse to the last records, you will notice that the number of records has been reduced to 636 as shown below.

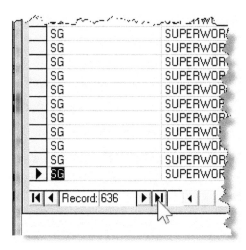

e. Once you have selected the fields, click on this icon 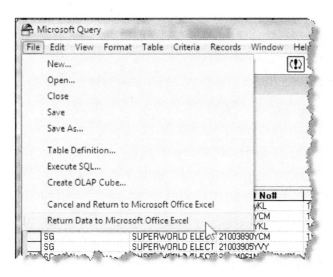 to exit the MS Query and return to Excel. Alternatively, you can also go to the menu and select **File → Return Data to Microsoft Office Excel**.

f. Select cell A1 as the cell to put the data; click on the **Properties** button.

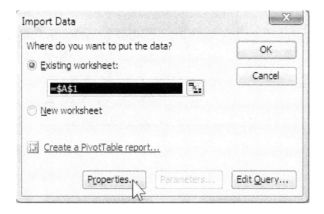

g. Select the options below including **Insert cells for new data, delete unused cells**. Click **OK**.

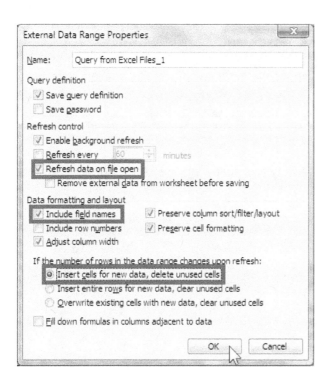

Insert Cells for new data, delete unused cells

This option will move the cells below the data down for the new data. Delete unused cells means they will move the cells below the data up.

Insert entire rows for new data, clear unused cells

Insert an entire row for the new data and keep the empty cells when the data is cleared.

Overwrite existing cells with new data, clear unused cells

Write the new data onto the rows below, even if there are data in those cells. Clear the content in the cells when the number of records in the database shrinks.

13.3 Add records from subsequent data sources

The steps are similar but not the same as that given for the 1st data source. Subsequent data sources, i.e. the second, third, fourth data source and so on will use the same approach given below.

a.   Select the cell in column A on the empty row following the last record presented by the first data source, **SG$.**

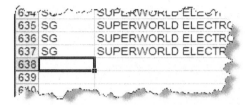

b.   From the Main Menu, select **Data → Import External Data → New Database Query**.

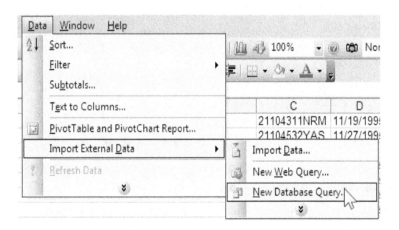

c.   Select **Excel Files** as the data source and click **OK**.

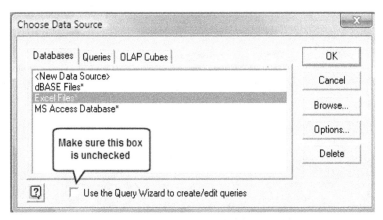

d.   In the next dialog box titled "**Select Workbook**", choose the file you want to work with.
      For our case, the name is **Consolidate data from diff workbooks.xls** and click **OK**.

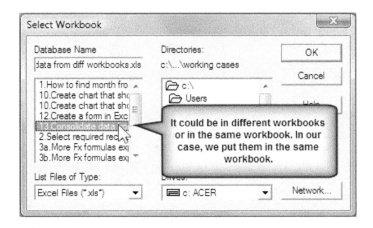

e.   In the **Add Tables** box, select the first file **CH$** and click Add before closing the dialog box.

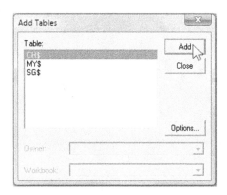

f.   Double Click on the * sign to present all the fields.

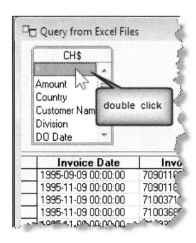

g.   Once you have selected the fields, click on this icon  to exit the MS Query and return to Excel. Alternatively, you can also go to the menu and select **File → Return Data to Microsoft Office Excel**.

h. Cell A638 was automatically displayed because we have pre-selected the cell after the last record from the first data source. If you prefer, you can highlight the range with a colour of your choice so that you know where the second data records starts. Next, click on the **Properties** button.

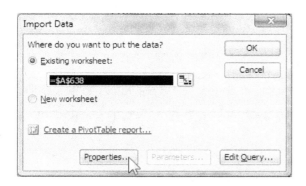

i. In the dialog box, check off the option **Include Field names**. Also select the option **Insert cells for new data, delete unused cells** as well as **Refresh data on file open**. Click **OK**.

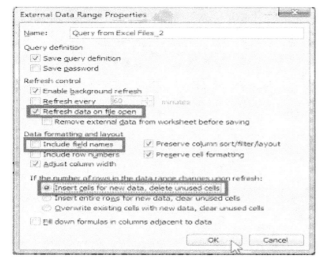

j. Repeat the above section for the subsequent data sources (MY). Now we have 3 data sources consolidated into one worksheet.

13.4 Create a name for the range

Now that we have consolidated the data from different files into one, we can create pivot tables and charts easily from the data.

The steps of creating a pivot table is very similar to **Case 4** except that we are uncertain of is the number of rows (data range) the list has. The number of rows fluctuates monthly whereas in **case 4**, the data range is fixed.

When we refresh the pivot table, Excel will update the changes you have made to the existing records. However, it will not automatically update the pivot table with new records inserted into the database subsequently.

One of the ways users get around this is by inserting rows before the last row.

Another way is using **Dynamic Range**. This is a good option if you are setting up the template for someone who is not familiar with pivot tables.

Firstly, they might not follow you instruction no matter how much you emphasize.

Secondly, they might forget the instruction even if they heard them initially. When they realised that the pivot table is providing inaccurate results, they will walk away and never look back.

To set up a dynamic range, you need to know the (*f*x) **OFFSET** formula, (*f*x) **COUNTA** formula (which has similar usage in **case 11**) and naming the range.

Why do we have to create a name for the range?

In step 2 of Pivot table wizard, we are required to enter a range into the box. But the wizard can only accept a static range e.g. A1:Z100 and a range name but not a formula. And range name can accept formulas. Therefore, we can use named range to store our formula and use it in the Pivot Table Wizard.

a.   Enter the following (*f*x) **OFFSET** formula in Cell F2
      =Offset(A1,0,0,1,1)

184

The (*f*x) **OFFSET** formula returns a cell or range reference using another cell as a benchmark. It works like a relative cell referencing.

e.g. =Offset(A1,0,0,1,1)

Using this (*f*x) **OFFSET** formula for explanation,

Cell **A1**, **=Offset(A1,0,0,1,1)** is the starting point.

The two **0**s, **=Offset(A1,0,0,1,1)** indicates that the target cell reference is zero row and zero column from cell A1. This means that the target cell reference begins in cell A1.

The two **1**s, **=Offset(A1,0,0,1,1)** indicates that the reference is one row high and one column wide. This means that the entire offset formula **=Offset(A1,0,0,1,1)** refers to cell A1. If we change two 1s into two 2s, the target reference would become a range e.g. **=A1:B2**. In the illustration below, the target reference would be A1:B4.

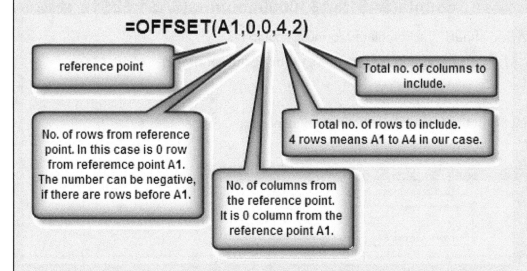

To test the formula, press the function ![F5] key (**Go To** function) and enter the entire formula including the equal sign ("=") into the reference area. Click OK. Excel will highlight the range A1:B4.

b. To make a dynamic range, we include the (*fx*) **COUNTA** formula in the (*fx*) **OFFSET** formula to automatically count the number of columns and rows we want to include in our range.

The (*fx*) **COUNTA** formula counts the number of **non-blank cells** within a range.

To count the number of rows to include, we can use =**Counta($B:$B)**.

To count the number of columns, we can use the following formula =**Counta($1:$1)**.

Note: Users are not allowed to enter any workings within this range. They will be included in the (fx) **COUNTA** *formula and return the wrong range.*

---

c. To include the (*fx*) **COUNTA** formula in the existing formula. Edit the cell as such =Offset($A$1,0,0,**counta($A$1:$A$10000),counta($A$1:$Z$1)**)). Since the data list is in sheet1, the completed formula should be

=Offset(sheet1!$A$1,0,0,Counta(sheet1!$A$1:$A$10000),Counta(sheet1!$A$1:$Z$1))

d. Highlight the entire formula, right click and select copy. Press [Esc] key.

e. At the Main Menu, select **Insert → Name → Define**.

186

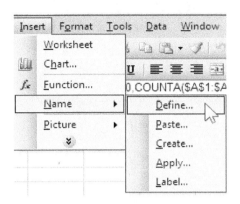

f. In the dialog box, enter a name for your pivot table data (in our case, we are using **pivot_table_data_source.** Paste the formula into the text box labelled **Refers to** as shown in the diagram below. Click the **Add** button to store the range name in the workbook.

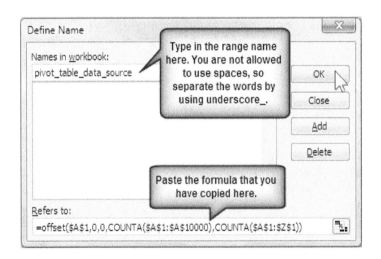

13.5 Automatically re-size the data range (Dynamic Range) for the pivot table

a. Select **Data → PivotTable and PivotChart Report**.

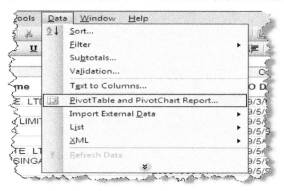

a. Select the **Microsoft Office Excel list or database** option and **Pivot Table** option and click **Next>**.

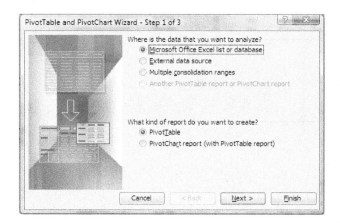

b. Enter in the name of the range that we defined earlier on i.e. **=pivot_table_data_source**

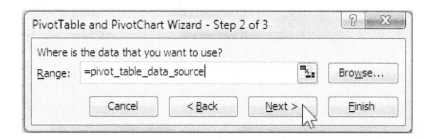

c. When you come to the wizard step 3 of 3, click on **Layout** button to include the fields you want. Follow through the wizard like in **Case 4.1**.

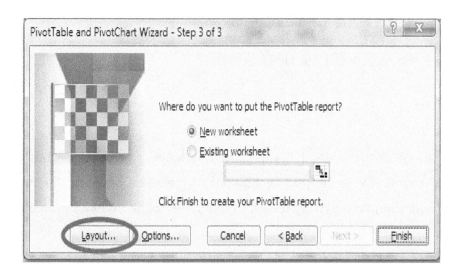

d. You can now enter new data in the data worksheet after the last row of your existing data. When you refresh the pivot table, the new data will be presented in the pivot table.

If you want to practise this case again, use the backup file named *Consolidate data from diff workbooks-backup.xls* to replace *Consolidate data from diff workbooks.xls* before starting all over again.

End of Case 13

Case 14: Compare Sales between 2 time periods

Key Learning Points: Use of the **calculated field** in pivot tables.

Case Study:

After a detailed review of your analysis for Period 1, your boss has a better grasp of the business situation. However, he would also prefer to see the fluctuations of the sales between the current and previous periods. It will help him monitor the business better. He hopes you can prepare the report for him.

With the detailed report in place, all you have to do is to add another column to include the difference between the periods using a function available in Pivot Table. Here is how.

Working Files:

14.Period 1.xls
14.Period 2.xls

Solution:

14.1 Setting up a workbook for consolidation

a.   Open the workbook named "14. Period 1.xls". Save the workbook as "Consol.xls". Rename the worksheet as "**consol**"

14.2 Create a name for the range

We can create pivot tables and charts easily from the data.

The steps of creating a pivot table is very similar to **Case 4** except that we are uncertain of is the number of rows (data range) the list has. The number of rows fluctuates monthly whereas in **case 4**, the data range is fixed.

When we refresh the pivot table, Excel will update the changes you have made to the existing records. However, it will not automatically update the pivot table with new records inserted into the database subsequently.

One of the ways users get around this is by inserting rows before the last row.

Another way is using **Dynamic Range**. This is a good option if you are setting up the template for someone who is not familiar with pivot tables.

Firstly, they might not follow you instruction no matter how much you emphasize.

Secondly, they might forget the instruction even if they heard them initially. When they realized that the pivot table is providing inaccurate results, they will walk away and never look back.

To set up a dynamic range, you need to know the (*fx*) *OFFSET* formula, (*fx*) *COUNTA* formula and naming the range.

Why do we have to create a name for the range?

In step 2 of Pivot table wizard, we are required to enter a range into the box. But the wizard can only accept a static range e.g. A1:Z100 and a range name but not a formula. And range name can accept formulas. Therefore, we can use named range to store our formula and use it in the Pivot Table Wizard.

b.   Enter the following (*f*x) *OFFSET* formula in Cell S2
      =Offset(A1,0,0,1,1)

The (*f*x) *OFFSET* formula returns a cell or range reference using another cell as a benchmark. It works like a relative cell referencing.

e.g. =Offset(A1,0,0,1,1)

Using this (*f*x) *OFFSET* formula for explanation,

Cell **A1**, **=Offset(A1,0,0,1,1)** is the starting point.

The two **0**s, **=Offset(A1,0,0,1,1)** indicates that the target cell reference is zero row and zero column from cell A1. This means that the target cell reference begins in cell A1.

The two **1**s, **=Offset(A1,0,0,1,1)** indicates that the reference is one row high and one column wide. This means that the entire offset formula **=Offset(A1,0,0,1,1)** refers to cell A1. If we change two 1s into two 2s, the target reference would become a range e.g. **=A1:B2**. In the illustration below, the target reference would be A1:B4.

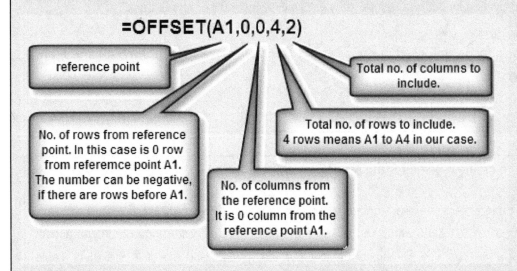

To test the formula, press the function [F5] key (**Go To** function) and enter the entire formula including the equal sign ("=") into the reference area. Click OK. Excel will highlight the range A1:B4.

192

c.   To make a dynamic range, we include the *(fx) COUNTA* formula in the *(fx) OFFSET* formula to automatically count the number of columns and rows we want to include in our range.

The *(fx) COUNTA* formula counts the number of **non-blank cells** within a range.

To count the number of rows to include, we can use =**Counta($B:$B)**.

To count the number of columns, we can use the following formula =**Counta($1:$1)**.

Note: Users are not allowed to enter any workings within this range. They will be included in the (fx) COUNTA formula and return the wrong range.

---

d.   To include the *(fx) COUNTA* formula in the existing formula. Edit the cell as such =Offset($A$1,0,0,**counta($A$1:$A$10000),counta($A$1:$Z$1)**)).   Verify that the formula is valid by using the Goto Function.

e.   Highlight the entire formula, right click and select copy. Press [Esc] key.

f.   At the Main Menu, select **Insert → Name → Define**.

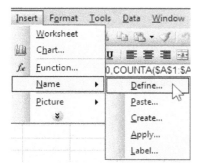

193

g. In the dialog box, enter a name for your pivot table data (in our case, we are using **pivot_table_data_source.** Paste the formula into the text box labelled **Refers to** as shown in the diagram below. Click the **Add** button to store the range name in the workbook.

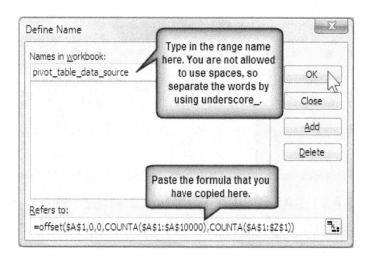

h. As you click on the add button, Excel will automatically add the worksheet name before the ranges. In the "refers to" box, the formula will become

=Offset(consol!$A$1,0,0,Counta(consol!$A$1:$A$10000),Counta(consol!$A$1:$Z$1))

14.3 Automatically re-size the data range (Dynamic Range) for the pivot table

a. Select **Data → PivotTable and PivotChart Report**.

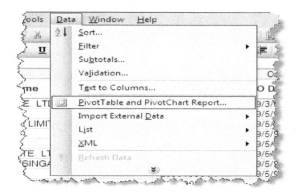

194

b.	Select the **Microsoft Office Excel list or database** option and **Pivot Table** option and click **Next>**.

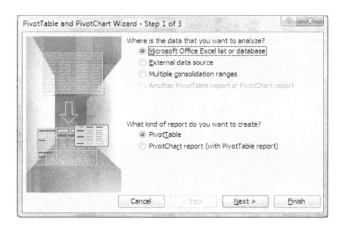

c.	Enter in the name of the range that we defined earlier on i.e. **=pivot_table_data_source**

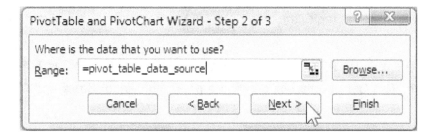

d. When you come to the wizard step 3 of 3, click on **Layout** button to include the fields you want. Follow through the wizard like in **Case 4.1**.

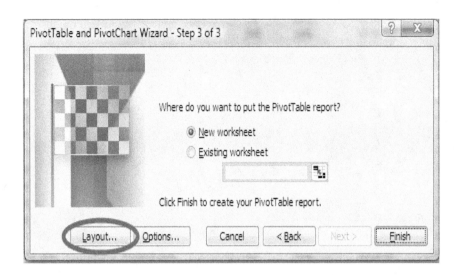

e. You can now enter new data in the data worksheet after the last row of your existing data. When you refresh the pivot table, the new data will be presented in the pivot table.

f. Add a new field called **previous period** in the **consol** worksheet and copy the **amount** column to this column. This set of data will be for the previous period. **Save** and **Close** the file.

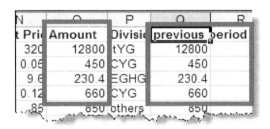

14.4 Consolidate the data for the second period

a. Open the workbook named "**14.Period 2.xls**"

b. Transfer the data from the **Sheet1** worksheet (in "14.Period 2.xls" workbook) to the **consol** worksheet ("in Consol.xls") starting from the row below the first/previous period data.

c. Add a new column and name it as **current period**. Copy the amount into this column.

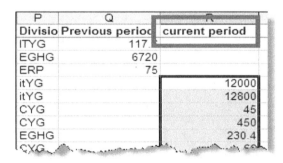

d. In **Sheet2** worksheet, right click in the pivot table and select **refresh data**.

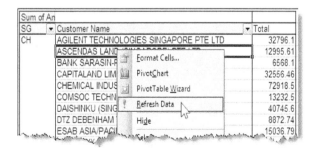

14.5 Setup the Pivot Table for comparison

a. Right click in the pivot table and select **Pivot Table wizard**.

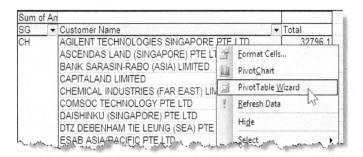

b. Click on the **Layout** button.

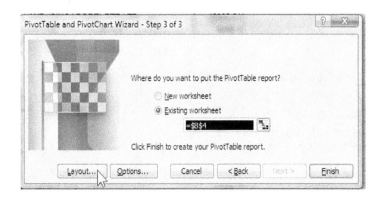

c. Add the fields **Current Period** and **Previous Period** into the data area and remove the **Amount** field. Click OK, then Finish to get out of the wizard

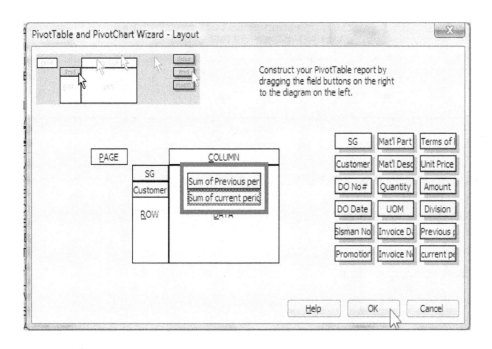

d. To present the sales for the 2 periods side by side, you need to drag and drop the Data field into the cell containing the word "**Total**": Point your cursor at the Data field. Click and hold on to the left mouse button. Move the mouse to the cell containing the word "Total". When you see a box with dotted line around the word "Total", let go of the left mouse button. The 2 periods are now presented side by side.

e. The data will be presented as follows:

	Data	
	Sum of Previous period	Sum of current period
E PTE LTD	32796.1	32796.1
LTD	12995.61	12995.61
	6568.1	6568.1
	32556.46	32556.46
ITED	72918.5	72918.5

14.6 Highlight the differences between the 2 periods.

a. Right click in the pivot table and select **Show PivotTable Toolbar**.

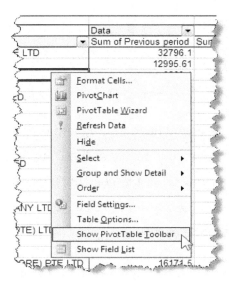

b. The Pivot Table toolbar appears.

c.   Select a cell in the pivot table. On the Pivot Table toolbar, click on the dropdown arrow next to the **Pivot Table** label, select **Formulas -> Calculated Field**.

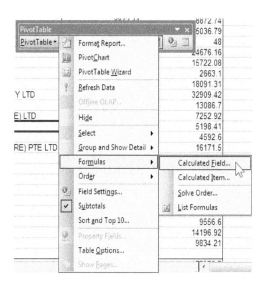

d.   In the **Name** box, type in the word **Exception**. Click on the **Formula** box, move the cursor to the **Fields** list and double click on the field "**Previous period**". The formula box will display **='Previous period'**. Type in the minus sign "**-**". Then, double click on the field **current period**. Click **Add** and **OK**.

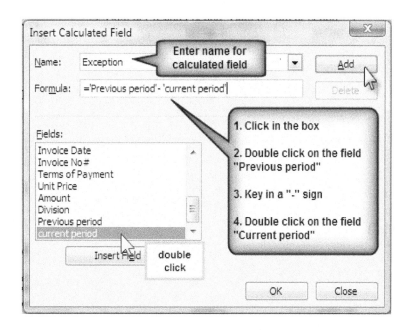

e.   The calculated field will be presented as follows:

Data	▼		
▼ Sum of Previous period	Sum of current perio	Sum of Exception
32796.1	32796.1	0
12995.61	12995.61	0
6568.1	6568.1	0
32556.46	32556.46	0
72918.5	72918.5	0

f.   You can now use the exception column to quickly identify changes in the amount between the previous period and current period.

End of Case 14

Case 15:   An Inventory Management System

Key Learning Points: **Data Validation** function, (*f*x) **OFFSET** formula, (*f*x) **MATCH** formula, (*f*x) **COUNTA** formula.

Case Study:

You have joined a new company as a logistic analyst. Your job responsibility is to keep track of the stocks movement in and out of the company. Due to expansion, your company has added a few distribution points. Each distribution point receives goods from the vendor directly and delivers the stocks to the customers they order. You are required to keep track of the stock level in all the distribution points and report on their performance weekly. You hope to use Excel to create an inventory system for each distribution point to facilitate your monitoring of the stocks at these distribution points and for your reporting even if it is on a daily basis.

Working Files:

15.An inventory mgmt system.xls
15.An inventory mgmt system-soln.xls

Solution:

15.1 Create a dropdown list for the product categories

a.   Select cell B15 in the **List** worksheet. At the Main Menu, select **Data → Validation**.

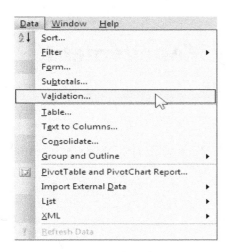

b.   In the **Data Validation** dialog box, select the **Settings** tab. In the **validation criteria**, **Allow** section, choose **List**. In the **Source** section, enter the range **=$A$1:$G$1**.

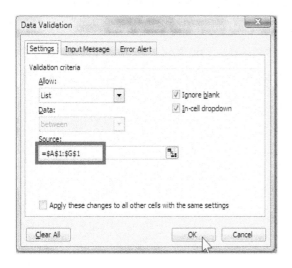

c.   Cell B15 now has a dropdown list of the product names.

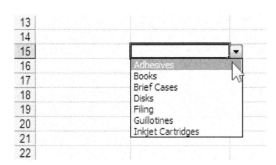

There are 3 ways:

1.   Type in the list using comma to separate them (e.g. Adhesive, Books, Brief Cases).

2.   Select the range that contains the list (e.g. A1:A5). You can only use a range in the same worksheet as the data validation entry.

3.   Create a list and put a name to the range. Using this method, you can place the list in another worksheet different from the data validation entry.

15.2 Create a dropdown list that changes based on the product categories selected

a.   To minimise data entry error, we will create a product list that is dependent on the product category selected using data validation and the (fx) OFFSET formula.

The (fx) OFFSET formula returns a cell or range reference using another cell as a benchmark. It works like a relative cell referencing.

e.g. =Offset(A1,0,0,1,1)

Using this (fx) OFFSET formula for explanation,
Cell A1, =Offset(A1,0,0,1,1) is the starting point.
The two 0s, =Offset(A1,0,0,1,1) indicates that the target cell reference is zero row and zero column from cell A1. This means that the target cell reference begins in cell A1.
The two 1s, =Offset(A1,0,0,1,1) indicates that the reference is one row high and one column wide. This means that the entire offset formula =Offset(A1,0,0,1,1) refers to cell A1. If we change two 1s into two 2s, the target reference would become =A1:B2. In the illustration below, the target reference would be A1:B4.

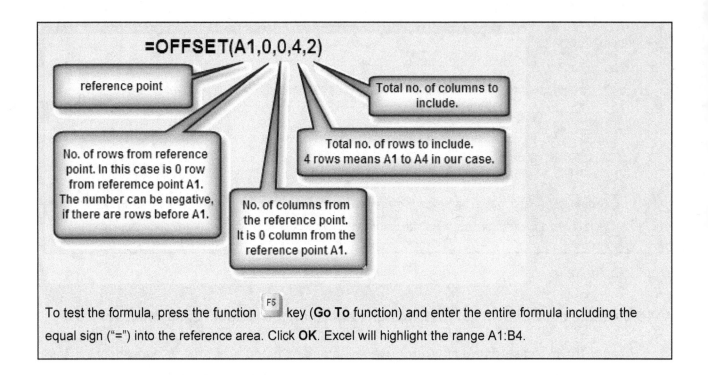

=OFFSET(A1,0,0,4,2)

reference point

Total no. of columns to include.

No. of rows from reference point. In this case is 0 row from referemce point A1. The number can be negative, if there are rows before A1.

Total no. of rows to include. 4 rows means A1 to A4 in our case.

No. of columns from the reference point. It is 0 column from the reference point A1.

To test the formula, press the function [F5] key (**Go To** function) and enter the entire formula including the equal sign ("=") into the reference area. Click **OK**. Excel will highlight the range A1:B4.

b. In cell C15 of the **List** worksheet, enter the formula **=Offset($A$1,1,0,5,1)**, the data validation will return the list in the range A2:A6. If we change the 2nd One in the (*fx*) **OFFSET** formula to 2 (=Offset($A$1,1,**1**,5,1)), the range will change to B2:B6 and so on.

=Offset($A$1,1,1,5,1)

c. To make the formula dependent on the entry in Cell B15, we need to make the 1 in (=Offset($A$1,1,**1**,5,1)), interactive, i.e. change according to the description in Cell B15. The (*fx*) **MATCH** formula will do the job.

206

The (fx) **MATCH** formula will return the relative position of value in a list made up of one column or one row.
=Match(B15,$A$1:$Z$1,1)

The (fx) **MATCH** formula consist of 3 parts:

Part 1 refers to the value/text we wish to match. In our case, the value is contained in cell B15.

Part 2 defines the range to look up for the value/text. . If the text is found in the first entry in the range, then the value of 1 is returned. In our example, we want to match the value in B15 in the range $A$1:$Z$1.

Part 3 is an optional input. The value of zero will make sure that an exact match is found. If the value of 1 is entered, it will find the value that is smaller than the match and closest to the match value. The values in the range must be arranged in ascending order. If the value of -1 is entered, it will find the value that is bigger than the match value, with the range arranged in descending order.

d.   Replace the 1 in (fx) **OFFSET** formula (=Offset($A$1,1,**1**,5,1)) with the (fx) **MATCH** formula (=**Match(B15,$A$1:$Z$1,1)**). Because the (fx) **OFFSET** formula starts from zero while the (fx) **MATCH** formula start from one, we have to minus 1 to the (fx) **MATCH** formula to align the 2 formulas. You will get the formula as follows:

=Offset($A$1,1, Match(B15,$A$1:$Z$1,1)-1,5,1)

=OFFSET($A$1,1,Match(B15,$A$1:$Z$1,1)-1,,5,1)

e.   Right click and copy the formula, press [Esc] key when done.

f.   Click on cell C15. At the Main Menu, select **Data → Validation**.

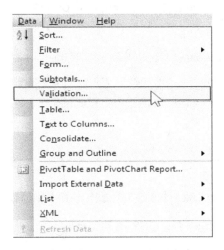

g.   In the **Data Validation** dialog box, select the **Settings** tab. In the **validation criteria**, **Allow** section, choose **List**. In the **Source** section, paste the formula.

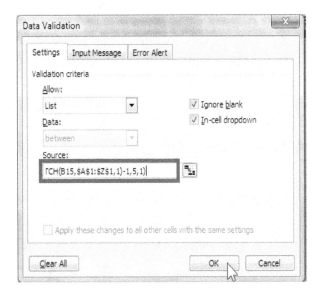

h.   Now the dropdown list in cell C15 is dependent on cell B15.

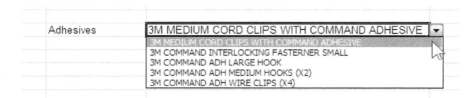

i.   The formula works only when the cell to be validated is in the same worksheet as the formula references. To make reference to the list from another worksheet, we have to label the formula with a name.

15.3 Assign a name to a range/formula

a.   Copy the formula from the data validation dialog box. Select the cell C15 in **List** worksheet. At the Main Menu, select **Data → Validation**.

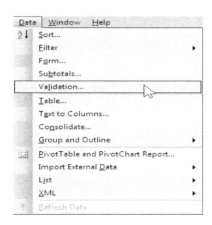

b. Highlight the formula at the **Source** section, copy (press  Ctrl key + letter C key together) the formula displayed. Click **Cancel** to exit.

c. At the Main Menu, select **Insert → Name → Define**.

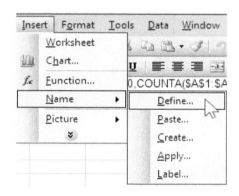

d. In the dialog box, enter a meaningful name (In this example, let's use the name **list2**.) Paste the formula (press Ctrl key + letter V key together) into the text box labelled **Refers to** as shown. Click **Add** to add the name to the list. Click **OK** to exit.

e. Repeat the entire process to create another name for the range referenced to the 1st dropdown list in cell B15, give the name as **list1**.

15.4 Making the 2 dropdown lists work in another worksheet

a. In the **Data** worksheet, select Cell B37. At the Main Menu, select **Data → Validation**.

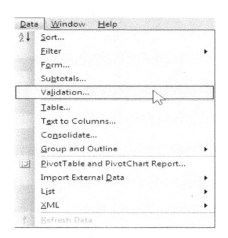

b.   In the **Data Validation** dialog box, select the **Settings** tab. In the **validation criteria**, **Allow** section, choose **List**. In the **Source** section, enter **=list2**. Click **OK**.

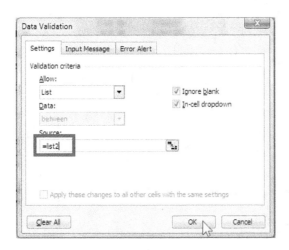

c.   Go to Cell A37 in the **Data** worksheet and create another data validation using the range named **list1**.

d.   At the Main Menu, select **Insert → Name → Define**.

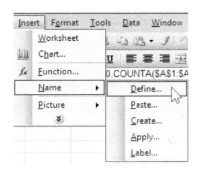

e.   The **(ƒx) OFFSET** formula in range name **list2** needed to be changed slightly because cell B15, which is the first dropdown list is in the **List** worksheet. Now, we want to refer to the dropdown list in the **Data** worksheet.

=OFFSET(list!$A$1,1, Match(**list**!B15,list!$A$1:$Z$1,1)-1,5,1)   to

=Offset(list!$A$1,1, Match(**Data**!B15,list!$A$1:$Z$1,1)-1,5,1)

212

f.   Copy the range A37:B37 down to populate the cells with the data validation settings.

36	Inkjet Cartridges	HYGENEX PRESTIGE KITCHEN TOWEL 2 PLY 60 SHEET
37	Adhesives	
38		3M MEDIUM CORD CLIPS WITH COMMAND ADHESIVE
39		3M COMMAND INTERLOCKING FASTERNER SMALL
40		3M COMMAND ADH LARGE HOOK
41		3M COMMAND ADH MEDIUM HOOKS (X2)
		3M COMMAND ADH WIRE CLIPS (X4)
42		

15.5 The Second dropdown list changes according to the number of entries in the list

a.   Currently, the (*fx*) **OFFSET** formula range up to 5 rows in the **List** worksheet determined by the 2nd last input in the formula

=Offset(list!$A$1,1, Match(Data!A37,list!$A$1:$Z$1,1)-1,**5**,1)

b.   To make the list changes according to the number of entries in the list, we can use the (*fx*) **COUNTA** formula. To count the number of records in range A2 to A100, we can use the formula

=Counta(List!A1:A100)

c.   Like the (*fx*) **OFFSET** formula, we need to identify which column we need to do the count. Therefore, we need to replace the **list!A1:A100** range with the offset formula we have created in earlier part. The (*fx*) **COUNTA** formula is now:

=Counta(Offset(List!$A$1,1,Match(Data!A37,List!$A$1:$Z$1,0)-1,5,1))

d.   We need to count the number of entries for 100 rows. Therefore we need to change the 5 in the formula to 100.

=Counta(Offset(List!$A$1,1,Match(Data!A37,List!$A$1:$Z$1,0)-1,**100**,1))

e.   Combined this (*fx*) **COUNTA** formula with the main (*fx*) **OFFSET** cum (*fx*) **MATCH** formula as shown below:

213

=Offset(List!\$A\$1,1,Match(Data!A37,List!\$A\$1:\$Z\$1,0)-1,Counta(Offset(List!\$A\$1,1, Match(B2,List!\$A\$1:\$Z\$1,0)-1,100,1)),1)

f.   Copy this formula and use it to replace the original formula defined in the named range **List2**.

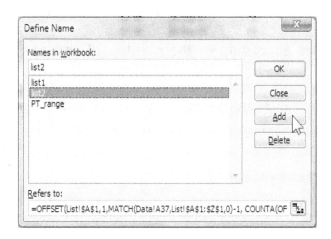

g.   Once set, try adding something in cell A37 of the **List** worksheet (e.g. 3M COMMAND ADH WIRE CLIPS (X6)), the second dropdown list in the Data worksheet will pick up the entry as well as change according to the input in the first dropdown list.

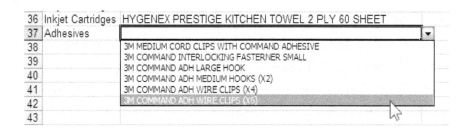

15.6 Create an intelligent range that resizes based the data list

a.   Using the (*f*x) **OFFSET** formula and the (*f*x) **COUNTA** formula, we could determine the size of the data list. Here is how:

b.   Enter the following (*f*x) **OFFSET** formula in Cell I2 of the **Data** worksheet. **=Offset(\$A\$1,0,0,1,1)**

c.   To identify the size of the data list, we can use the **(ƒx)** *COUNTA* formula to automatically count the number of columns and rows we need to include in our range.

The **(ƒx)** *COUNTA* formula counts the number of non-blank cells within a range.
To count the number of rows to include, we can use "counta($A:$A)".

To count the number of columns, we can use the following formula "counta($1:$1)"

Note: Users are not allowed to enter any workings within this range. It will be included in the counta formula and return the wrong range.

---

d.   Replace the first 1 in the offset formula with **Counta($A:$A)** to count the rows; replace the 2nd 1 in the offset formula with **Counta($1:$1)** to count the number of columns. The final formula should be

=Offset($A$1,0,0, **counta($A:$A)**, **counta($1:$1)**)

15.7 Create a name for the range to be used for the Pivot Table

---

Why do we have to create a name for the range?

In step 2 of Pivot table wizard, we are required to enter a range into the box. But the wizard can only accept a static range e.g. A1:Z100 and not a formula. But it is able to accept a range name. And range name can accept formulas. Therefore, we can use named range to get around the limitation set in the wizard.

---

a.   Select cell I2 of **Data** worksheet. Highlight and copy the formula displayed in the formula bar. Press the "Esc" Key when done.

b.   At the Main Menu, select **Insert → Name → Define**.

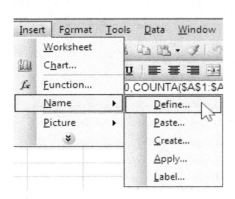

c.   In the dialog box, enter a meaningful name (In this example, let's use the name **PT_range**. Paste the formula (press [Ctrl] key + letter [V] key together) into the text box labelled Refers to as shown. Click the **Add** button to add the name to the list. Click **OK** to exit.

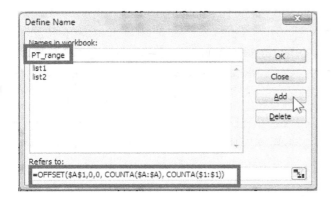

216

15.8 Create a Pivot table for the stock movement

a.   Select **Data → PivotTable and PivotChart Report**.

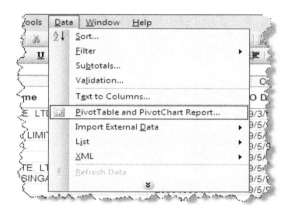

b.   Select the **Microsoft Office Excel list or database** option and **Pivot Table** option and click **Next>**.

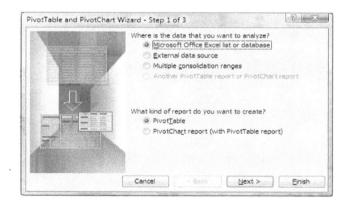

c.   Enter the name of the range **PT_range** after the equal sign. Click **Next>**.

d.   When you come to the wizard step 3 of 3, click on **Layout** button.

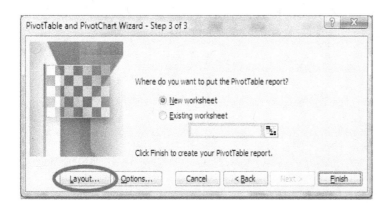

e.   ***Drag and drop*** the fields into the respective places as shown below and click **OK**.

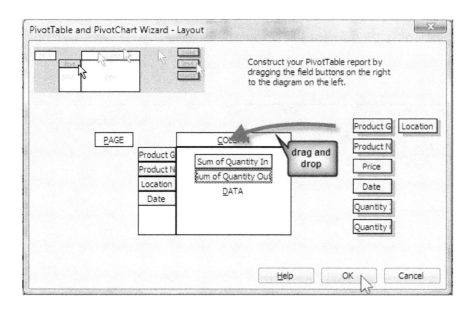

f.　Select the option to put the pivot Table on a new sheet and click **Finish.**

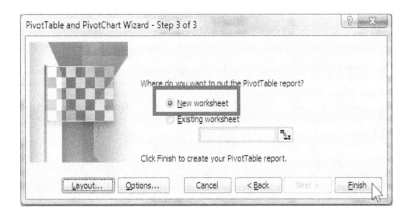

15.9 Showing the stock movement in Pivot Table

a.　In our example, we can calculate the net change between the "Quantity In" and "Quantity Out" by using the formula function in Pivot Table. You can only do this using the **Pivot Table Toolbar**.

b.　Right click within the pivot table. Select **Show Pivot Table Toolbar** (if the description is Hide Pivot Table Toolbar, it means that the toolbar is already displayed in Excel).

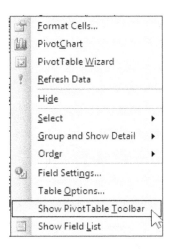

c.   The pivot table toolbar should become visible.

d.   Click on the label **Pivot Table** in the toolbar and from the dropdown menu, select
       Formulas → Calculated Field.

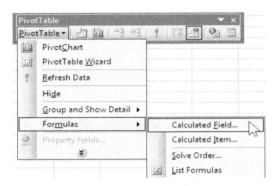

e.   In the **Name** box, type in the word **Net_Change**. Click on **the Formula** box, move to the
       Fields list and double click on the field **Quantity In**. Type in the minus sign "**-**". Then,
       double click on the field **Quantity Out**. Click **Add** and **OK**.

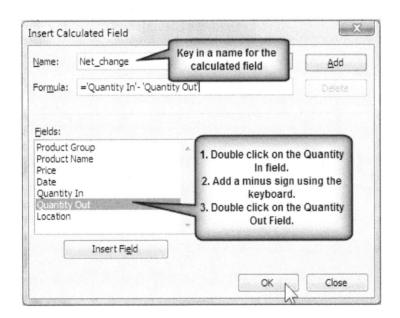

15.10 Changing the original Pivot Table Layout

a.   Right click on the pivot table and Select **PivotTable Wizard**.

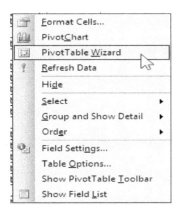

b.   Click on the **layout** button.

c.   Remove the fields **Sum of Quantity In** and **Sum of Quantity Out**. Click **OK** and in the next box, click **Finish**.

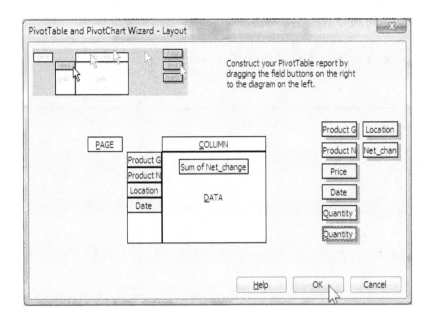

d.   Now the pivot table only show the net change of the stock movement.

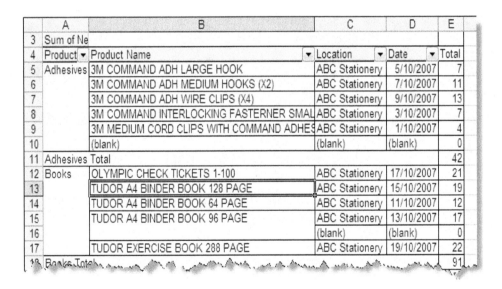

	A	B	C	D	E
3	Sum of Ne				
4	Product ▾	Product Name ▾	Location ▾	Date ▾	Total
5	Adhesives	3M COMMAND ADH LARGE HOOK	ABC Stationery	5/10/2007	7
6		3M COMMAND ADH MEDIUM HOOKS (X2)	ABC Stationery	7/10/2007	11
7		3M COMMAND ADH WIRE CLIPS (X4)	ABC Stationery	9/10/2007	13
8		3M COMMAND INTERLOCKING FASTERNER SMAL	ABC Stationery	3/10/2007	7
9		3M MEDIUM CORD CLIPS WITH COMMAND ADHES	ABC Stationery	1/10/2007	4
10		(blank)	(blank)	(blank)	0
11	Adhesives Total				42
12	Books	OLYMPIC CHECK TICKETS 1-100	ABC Stationery	17/10/2007	21
13		TUDOR A4 BINDER BOOK 128 PAGE	ABC Stationery	15/10/2007	19
14		TUDOR A4 BINDER BOOK 64 PAGE	ABC Stationery	11/10/2007	12
15		TUDOR A4 BINDER BOOK 96 PAGE	ABC Stationery	13/10/2007	17
16			(blank)	(blank)	0
17		TUDOR EXERCISE BOOK 288 PAGE	ABC Stationery	19/10/2007	22
18	Books Total				91

15.11 Summarise the Stock Movement by Month

a. Right click at the **Date** header/field, in the pop-up menu, select **Group and Show Detail**
→ **Group**.

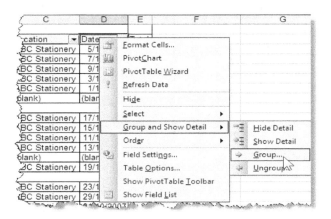

b. Excel will automatically select the full range of the dates you wish to group. Select the
groupings (month, quarter, year) you need. You can select more than 1. Click **OK**.

c.   The details are now summarised by Month.

	A	B	C	D	E
1					
2					
3	Sum of net				
4	Product ▼	Product Name ▼	Location ▼	Date ▼	Total
5	Adhesives	3M COMMAND ADH LARGE HOOK	ABC Stationery	Oct	7
6		3M COMMAND ADH MEDIUM HOOKS (X2)	ABC Stationery	Oct	11
7		3M COMMAND ADH WIRE CLIPS (X4)	ABC Stationery	Oct	13
8		3M COMMAND INTERLOCKING FASTERNE	ABC Stationery	Oct	7
9		3M MEDIUM CORD CLIPS WITH COMMAN	ABC Stationery	Oct	4
10	Adhesives Total				42
11	Books	OLYMPIC CHECK TICKETS 1-100	ABC Stationery	Nov	21

d.   Click and hold on to the date field and move to the Data area, drop it when you see a box outline covering the **Total** cell as shown.

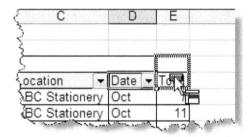

e.   Your stock movement is now presented across the columns by month.

C	D	E	F	G	H
	Date ▼				
Location ▼	Jul	Oct	Nov	Dec	Grand Total
ABC Stationery	0	7	0	0	7
ABC Stationery	0	11	0	0	11
ABC Stationery	0	13	0	0	13
ABC Stationery	0	7	0	0	7
ABC Stationery	0	4	0	0	4
	0	42	0	0	42
ABC Stationery	0	0	21	0	21

15.12 Present the individual stock level by month

a. Double click on the **Sum of Net Change** data field located at the top left hand corner of the pivot table.

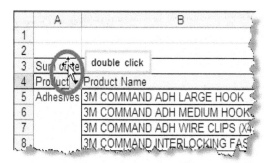

b. Click on the **Options** Button found in the **PivotTable Field** dialog box.

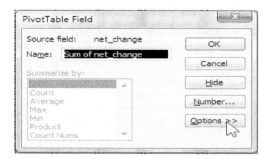

c. In the **Show data as** box, select **Running total in**.

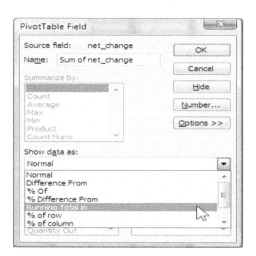

d.   In the **Base field**, select **Date**. Click **OK**.

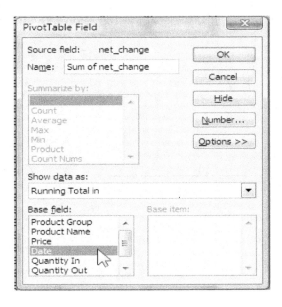

e.   The pivot table will now show the stock level by product for each month.

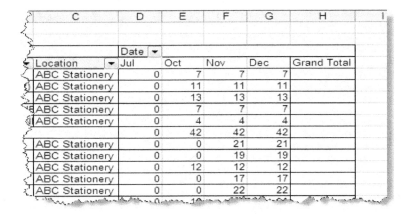

	C	D	E	F	G	H	I
		Date ▼					
Location	▼	Jul	Oct	Nov	Dec	Grand Total	
	ABC Stationery	0	7	7	7		
	ABC Stationery	0	11	11	11		
	ABC Stationery	0	13	13	13		
	ABC Stationery	0	7	7	7		
	ABC Stationery	0	4	4	4		
		0	42	42	42		
	ABC Stationery	0	0	21	21		
	ABC Stationery	0	0	19	19		
	ABC Stationery	0	12	12	12		
	ABC Stationery	0	0	17	17		
	ABC Stationery	0	0	22	22		

End of Case 15

Case 16:　Looking up prices for quotations

Key Learning Points:　**Data Validation** function, (*f*x) **OFFSET** formula, (*f*x) **MATCH** formula, (*f*x) **COUNTIF** formula, (*f*x) **VLOOKUP** formula, use of "**&**".

Case Study:

James is pre-sales consultant. He helps his clients develops business solutions using products and/or parts from different suppliers. When preparing quotation, he has to identify the parts used and the list prices.

He does this by search through multiple worksheets containing different categories of products. The search may return more than one result and he would have to choose one of them that match his requirement. He may have to do this many times for a quotation.

Working Files:

16.Looking up prices for quotations.xls
16.Looking up prices for quotation-soln.xls

Solution:

16.1 Create a dropdown list for the product numbers

a.　Create a dropdown list in a cell using the **Data Validation** function. Select the cell where you want the dropdown list to appear. In our case, it is Cell C4 in the **SampleBOM** worksheet.

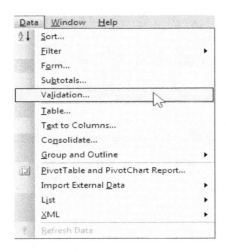

b.   At the Main Menu, select **Data → Validation**.

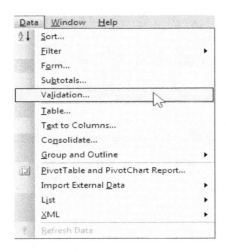

c.   In the **Data Validation** dialog box, select the **Settings** tab. In the **validation criteria**, **Allow** section, choose **List**. In the **Source** section, enter the product names (NS80-AUX, NS80-AUX-FD, NS80-C-DCD) into the source box.

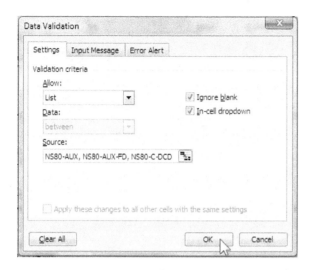

d. Now, cell C4 have a dropdown list for selection.

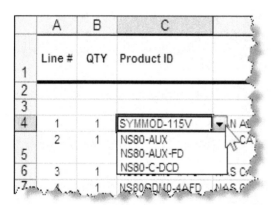

There are 3 ways to manage the entries in the dropdown list:

1. Type in the list using comma to separate them (e.g. Adhesive, Books, Brief Cases).

2. Select the range that contains the list (e.g. A1:A5). You can only use a range in the same worksheet as the data validation entry.

3. Create a list and put a name to the range. Using this method, you can place the list in another worksheet different from the data validation entry/dropdown box.

16.2 Assign a name to a range/formula

a.   Select the **Price_list** worksheet. Go to the Main Menu, select **Insert → Name → Define**.

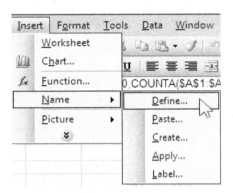

b.   Enter a meaningful name for the range. In this example, let's use the name **product_num**. In the **Refer to** box, select the range you want to label using your mouse. In this case, select the range A2:A49. Click **Add** to add the range name to the list. Click **Close**. **Note:** *make sure the range uses absolute reference.*

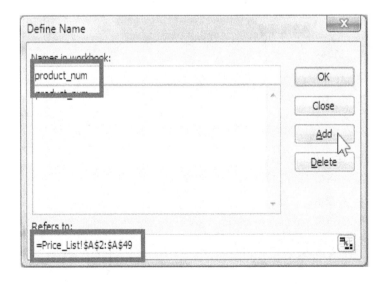

16.3 Use a range located in another worksheet for the dropdown list

a.   Using the range name, you could now set up the data validation list using the range from another worksheet. Select cell C4 of **SampleBOM** worksheet. At the Main Menu, select **Data → Validation**.

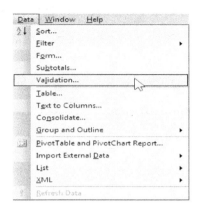

b. In the **Data Validation** dialog box, select the **Settings** tab. In the **validation criteria**, **Allow** section, choose **List**. In the **Source** section, enter **=product_num**. Click **OK**.

c.   Now, cell C4 have a dropdown list for selection. Using the range name, the list refers to range A2:A49 in the **Price_List** worksheet.

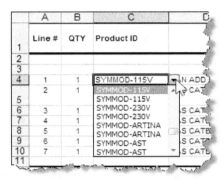

16.4 Making the Second dropdown list dependent on the first dropdown list

a.   For some product numbers, there is more than one item to choose from. For example, "SYMMOD-115V" refers to 2 different items, one in "NAS CATB" category and another in "SAN Add-On". Therefore, we need another dropdown list that could allow the user to select the product from the appropriate category.

b.   We can do that by using the following formulas: (fx) **OFFSET** formula, (fx) **MATCH** formula and (fx) **COUNTIF** formula.

The Concept

When a product number is entered, Excel must know where (the range) to look for the product number.

It then finds the first row that contains the product number. The list must be pre-sorted by product numbers.

Then count how many times the product number appears. This will allow us to determine how many categories contain the product number and include them in the list.

User can therefore select the appropriate category for the product.

---

c.   Select the cell D4 in the sampleBOM worksheet.

d. To define the range for Excel to look for the product category (i.e. "NAS CATB" or "SAN Add-On"), we can use the (fx) **OFFSET** formula.

The (fx) **OFFSET** formula returns a cell or range reference using another cell as a benchmark. It works like a relative cell referencing.

e.g. =Offset(A1,0,0,1,1)

Using this (fx) **OFFSET** formula for explanation,

Cell **A1**, **=Offset(A1,0,0,1,1)** is the starting point.

The two **0**s, **=Offset(A1,0,0,1,1)** indicates that the target cell reference is zero row and zero column from cell A1. This means that the target cell reference begins in cell A1.

The two **1**s, **=Offset(A1,0,0,1,1)** indicates that the reference is one row high and one column wide. This means that the entire offset formula **=Offset(A1,0,0,1,1)** refers to cell A1. If we change two 1s into two 2s, the target reference would become **=A1:B2**. In the illustration below, the target reference would be A1:B4.

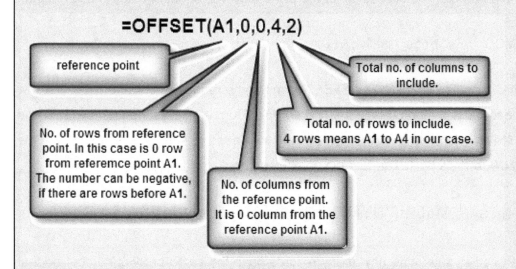

To test the formula, press the function [F5] key (**Go To** function) and enter the entire formula including the equal sign ("=") into the reference area. Click OK. Excel will highlight the range A1:B4.

---

e. To find the first row in which the product number appears, we could use the **(fx)** **MATCH** formula.

The **(fx)** **MATCH** formula will return the relative position of value in a list made up of one column or one row.

The **(fx)** **MATCH** formula consist of 3 parts:
Part 1 refers to the value/text we wish to match.

Part 2 defines the range to look up for the value/text. . If the text is found in the first entry in the range, then the value of 1 is returned.

Part 3 is an optional input. The value of zero will make sure that an exact match is found. If the value of 1 is entered, it will find the value that is equal or smaller but closest to the match value. The values in the range must be arranged in ascending order. If the value of -1 is entered, it will find the value that is equal or bigger than the match value, with the range arranged in descending order.

---

f. In our example, the lookup value is the product number "SYMMOD-115V". The product number in listed in Column A. Since we want an exact match, we should be put in zero for the 3rd parameter. Select cell G5 of the **price_list** worksheet and key in this formula

=Match("SYMMOD-115V",Price_List!$A:$A,0)

g. Putting this formula into the **(fx)** **OFFSET** formula, the range will start from the first row where the formula is found. Since the **(fx)** **OFFSET** formula treats the first row as 0 and the **(fx)** **MATCH** formula treat the 1st row as 1, we need to subtract the result from the **(fx)** **MATCH** formula by 1. The formula combined should be

=Offset(Price_List!$A$1,**Match("SYMMOD-115V",Price_List!$A:$A,0)-1**,0,1,1)

h. Next, we need to determine how many records have the same product number so that we could include them in the list/range. Using the **(fx)** **COUNTIF** formula, we could easily count the number of records sharing the same product number.

i.	The (*fx*) *COUNTIFf* formula is **=Countif($A:$A,"SYMMOD-115V").** Combined with the (*fx*) *OFFSET* formula, we will have

=Offset(Price_List!$A$1,Match("SYMMOD-115V",Price_List!$A:$A,0)-1,0,
Countif($A:$A,"SYMMOD-115V"),1)

j.	Since we want to display the product category instead of the product number, we could change the 0 (which is for the product number) to 1 (which is for product category). The formula will become

=Offset(Price_List!$A$1,Match("SYMMOD-115V",Price_List!$A:$A,0)-1,**1**,
Countif($A:$A,"SYMMOD-115V"),1)

k.	To re-use the formula for every row, we could replace the fixed product number with a relative cell reference like this

=Offset(Price_List!$A$1,Match(**sampleBOM!C4**,Price_List!$A:$A,0)-
1,1,Countif(Price_List!$A:$A,**sampleBOM!C4**),1)

fx	=OFFSET(price_list!$A$1,MATCH(sampleBOM!C4,price_list!$A:$A,0)-1,1,COUNTIF($A:$A,sampleBOM!C4),1)		
B	C	D	E

l.	Copy the above formula into Cell D4.

m.	Make sure that Cell D4 is selected. Then provide a name (**product_cat**) for this formula using the **Name** range function. At the Main Menu, select **Insert → Name → Define**.

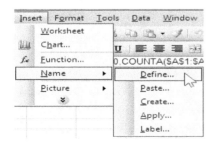

Note:
When the range name is defined, the active cell must be in Cell D4 because we have made a relative reference to cell C4.
The range name, when used in data validation, will always take the value to the left of the dropdown list. The relative reference rule applies in range names.

n. In the dialog box, enter **product_cat** as name. Paste the formula (press ![Ctrl] key +
letter ![V] key together) into the text box labelled Refers to as shown. Click **Add** to add
the name to the list. Click **OK** to exit.

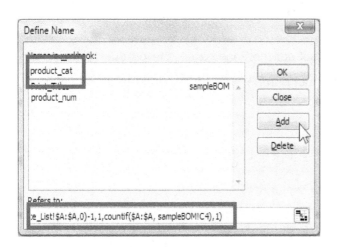

o. In cell D4 of the **sampleBOM** worksheet, set up another dropdown list in Data
Validation function using the range name **product_cat**.

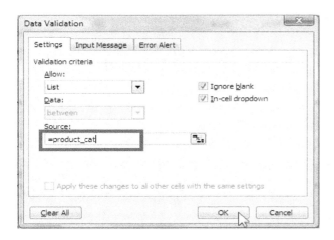

p. Now, the second list is dependent on the first list.

	A	B	C	D	
1	Line #	QTY	Product ID		Desc
2					
3					
4	1	1	SYMMOD-115V	NAS CATB ▼	80
	2	1	NS80CDM0-4A	NAS CATB	80.
5				SAN ADD ON	IM.
6	3	1	NS80CDM0-4A-JL	NAS CATB	NS80

16.5 Looking for a value using 2 conditions

a. The price of the product is retrieved using 2 values/text, the product number and product category. We could use the (ƒx) **VLOOKUP** formula for this task.

b. To lookup 2 values, we could combine them together using the ampersand ("&") or the (ƒx) **CONCATENATE** formula. Before we could lookup for the combined value, we have to create another column which list the combined values in the lookup table. We use the ampersand ("&") for this task.

The (ƒx) **CONCATENATE** formula joins several text strings into one text string. The text items can be text strings, numbers, or single-cell references. It works exactly the same as theampersand "&".

---

c. In cell C2 of the **Price_List** worksheet, enter the formula **=A2&B2**. This will combine the product number and product category into Cell C2. Copy the formula down the rows in column C.

	C2 ▼	ƒx =A2&B2		
	A	B	C	
1	Model #	Product Cat	Combined	Desc
2	NS80-AUX	NAS CATB	NS80-AUXNAS CATB	NS80
3	NS80-AUX-FD	NAS CATB	NS80-AUX-FDNAS CATB	NS80
4	NS80-C-DCD	NAS CATB	NS80-C-DCDNAS CATB	DOC &
5	NS80CDM0-4A	NAS CATB	NS80CDM0-4ANAS CATB	NS80
6	NS80CDM0-4AFD	NAS CATB	NS80CDM0-4AFDNAS CATB	NS80

237

d.   To look up the price, in the cell G4 of **SampleBOM** worksheet, enter the formula

=Vlookup(C4&D4,Price_List!$C$1:$E$49,3,FALSE)

e.   The price will appear when the relevant selection is made.

	G4		▼		*fx* =VLOOKUP(C4&D4,price_list!$C$1:$E$49,3,FALSE)		
	A	B	C	D	E	F	G
1	Line #	QTY	Product ID		Description	Units	List Unit Price (S$)
2							
3							
4	1	1	SYMMOD-115V	SAN ADD ON	NS80 GW ENCL WITH 2 XB60 FACTORY	EA	3000
	2	1	NS80CDMO-4A	NAS CATB	NS80 CONTROL STATION FACTORY PRIMA...	EA	

f.   Copy the formula to the rest of columns. With the formula, the unit price is displayed
      instantly.

Description	Units	List Unit Price (S$)	To Pri
NS80 GW ENCL WITH 2 XB60 FACTORY	EA	3,000.00	
NS80 CONTROL STATION FACTORY PRIMARY	EA	31,566.60	
NS80 XB60: 4GB6CU+2OP GW FACT	EA	41,037.10	
NS80 ENCLOSURE FACTORY	EA	40,470.00	
DOC & CD: NS80+CLAR	EA	190,872.50	
DOC & CD: NS80	EA	190,872.50	
MODEM 230V	EA	190,872.50	
Hardware Sub-total			

End of Case 16

Case 17: Limit answers to a pre-defined list using Data Validation

Key Learning Points: **Data Validation** function

Solution:

a. You can limit the user from entering information you do not want using data validation. Here is how:

b. Select cell B2 in a new worksheet. At the Main Menu, select **Data → Validation**.

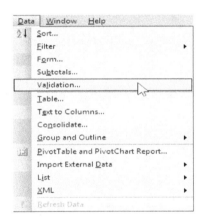

c. In the **Data Validation** dialog box, select the **Settings** tab. In the **validation criteria**, **Allow** section, choose **List**. In the **Source** section, enter the list of words or phrases allowed, each of them separated by a comma as shown

Depending on your needs, you could limit the user to only

1. Whole Number
2. Decimals
3. Date
4. Time
5. A number of characters or
6. A result based on a formula

d.   In the **Input Message** tab, you can enter a Title or a question and a message for the user.

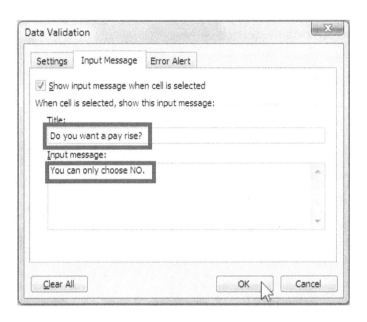

e.   In the **Error Alert** tab, enter a title and message if the user does not follow your instruction. Click **OK** to exit.

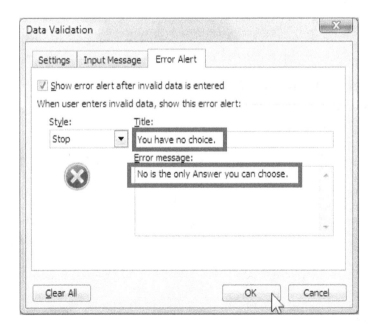

f.   In cell B2, the dropdown list only consists of NOs. If you try to overwrite it and key in **YES**, you will be prompted by a message.

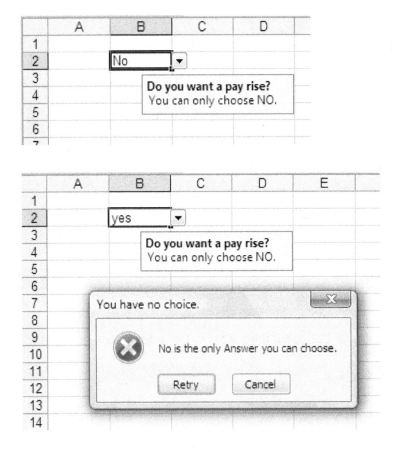

End of Case 17

Case 18: Conditional Formatting

Key Learning Points: **Conditional formatting** function.

Solution:

18.1 Format the cell based on the content within the cell

a.   Select cell B2 of a new worksheet.

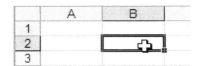

b.   At the Main Menu, select **Format → Conditional Format**.

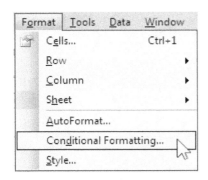

c.	In the dialog box, select the range for the cell value to activate the formatting to be between **1** and **2**. Set the format if the condition is satisfied. Click **Add** if you want to add another condition. You can have up to 3 conditions in the cell. Click **OK**.

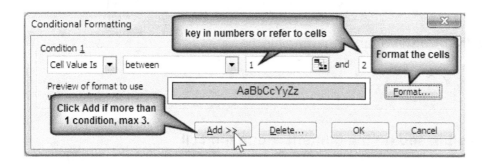

d.	Try entering values between 1 and 2 in cell B2, the cell will change its colour as the condition is met.

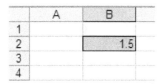

18.2 Format the cell based on the content of another cell(s)

a.	Select cell A2 of a new worksheet.

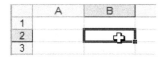

b.	At the Main Menu, select **Format → Conditional Formatting**.

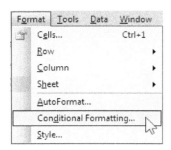

c. In the dialog box, change the option **Cell Value is** to **Formula is.** Enter a formula as a condition. In our case, we shall enter **B2>F2**. Format the cell as wish. Click **Add** if you want to add more conditions. Click **OK**.

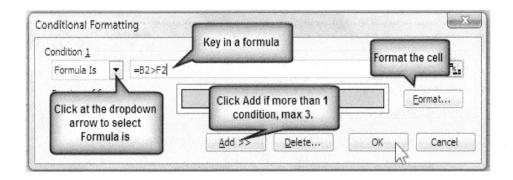

d. Try entering figures in cell B2 and cell F2, if the condition of B2 > F2 is met, the cell B2 will change its colour.

	A	B	C	D	E	F
1						
2		2				1
3						
4						

End of Case 18

Appendix

1. *Commonly used worksheet functions*

1.1   Date and Time

i.   <u>DATE</u>   Returns the serial number of a particular date

ii.   <u>DATEVALUE</u>   Converts a date in the form of text to a serial number

iii.   <u>DAY</u>   Converts a serial number to a day of the month

iv.   <u>MONTH</u>   Converts a serial number to a month

v.   <u>TIMEVALUE</u>   Converts a time in the form of text to a serial number

vi.   <u>WEEKDAY</u>   Converts a serial number to a day of the week

vii.   <u>WEEKNUM</u>   Converts a serial number to a number representing where the week falls numerically with a year

viii. <u>YEAR</u>   Converts a serial number to a year

1.2   Information

i.   <u>COUNTBLANK</u>   Counts the number of blank cells within a range

ii.   <u>ISBLANK</u>   Returns TRUE if the value is blank

iii.   <u>ISERR</u>   Returns TRUE if the value is any error value except #N/A

iv.   <u>ISERROR</u>   Returns TRUE if the value is any error value

v.   <u>ISNA</u>   Returns TRUE if the value is the #N/A error value

vi.   <u>ISNUMBER</u>   Returns TRUE if the value is a number

vii.   <u>ISREF</u>   Returns TRUE if the value is a reference

1.3   Logical

i.   <u>AND</u>   Returns TRUE if all its arguments are TRUE

ii.   <u>IF</u>   Specifies a logical test to perform

iii.   <u>OR</u>   Returns TRUE if any argument is TRUE

246

1.4 Lookup and Reference

i. CHOOSE   Chooses a value from a list of values

ii. COLUMN   Returns the column number of a reference

iii. HLOOKUP   Looks in the top row of an array and returns the value of the indicated cell

iv. INDEX   Uses an index to choose a value from a reference or array

v. LOOKUP   Looks up values in a vector or array

vi. OFFSET   Returns a reference offset from a given reference

vii. VLOOKUP   Looks in the first column of an array and moves across the row to return the value of a cell

1.5 Math and Trigonometry

i. ROUND   Rounds a number to a specified number of digits

ii. ROUNDDOWN   Rounds a number down, toward zero

iii. ROUNDUP   Rounds a number up, away from zero

iv. MOD   Returns the remainder from division

v. SUMIF   Adds the cells specified by a given criteria

vi. TRUNC   Truncates a number to an integer

1.6 Statistical

vii. COUNT   Counts the number of cells within a range that contains value

viii. COUNTA   Counts the number of cells within a range that are not blanks. A space is NOT considered a blank

1.7 Text and Data

i. CONCATENATE   Joins several text items into one text item

ii. FIND   Finds one text value within another (case-sensitive)

iii. SEARCH   Finds one text value within another (not case-sensitive)

iv. LEFT   Returns the leftmost characters from a text value

v. LEN   Returns the number of characters in a text string

vi.   <u>LOWER</u>   Converts text to lowercase

vii.   <u>MID</u>   Returns a specific number of characters from a text string starting at the position you specify

viii.   <u>PROPER</u>   Capitalizes the first letter in each word of a text value

ix.   <u>RIGHT</u>   Returns the rightmost characters from a text value

x.   <u>T</u>   Converts its arguments to text

xi.   <u>TEXT</u>   Formats a number and converts it to text

xii.   <u>TRIM</u>   Removes spaces from text

xiii.   <u>UPPER</u>   Converts text to uppercase

xiv.   <u>VALUE</u>   Converts a text argument to a number

2. *Install MS Query*

MS Query is a simple but powerful ad-hoc query tool that you can use to retrieve and organize data from databases (such as Access, SQL database server, Dbase, or even Excel worksheets, just to name a few). The retrieved data can be displayed directly on a MS Excel worksheet for further editing or be presented in a pivot table or pivot chart report or just as list of records. The feature is readily available in MSOffice but not installed in the standard setup. Here is one way to install MSQuery:

a.   Get ready your MSOffice installation CDs and open up Excel Application.

b.   Go to the Main Menu, **Data → PivotTable and PivotChart Report.**

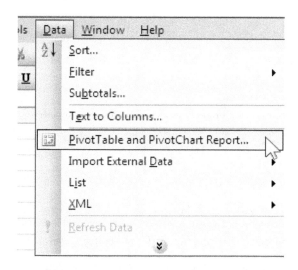

c. Select **External data source**, **Pivot table** as shown and click **Next>**.

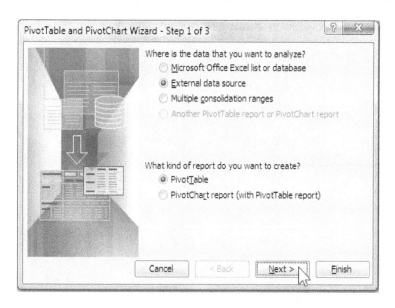

d. Click **Get Data** in the next step.

e. If MS Query is not installed, Excel will prompt you and asked if you wish to install MS Query. Click **Yes** and insert the MSOffice installation disk when necessary.

f. MS Query would have been installed in your computer. You can continue with the wizard to create your pivot table or database query. Alternatively, you can also click **Cancel** to exit.

THE END

Sales Performance Analytics

with Excel

Achieve breakthrough performance in Sales/Marketing like never before

"The Excel Pivot Table combined with MS Query are fantastic tools! I used them to extract the required data from ACCPAC and submit it to my Organisation's HQ in Germany. I recommended your course to one of my business associates who claims to work a lot with Excel and databases. When I showed him how quickly I could sort out the databases with for example VLOOKUP of the Industry Class, he was SOLD! Thanks for your Excel course plus your guidance!"

Bilal
Managing Director
Igus Singapore Pte Ltd

Excel remains an important business application as many companies & most sales and marketing personnel manage their data in Excel files. The popularity of Excel is obvious. It offers familiar features such as bulk copy & paste, formulas, lookup & formatting functions. Spreadsheets are a convenient way for many business users to create and maintain their sales performance data. Additionally, Excel has a format that is easily transferable and makes sharing of data between individuals and organizations easy.

Depending on how conversant you are in using Excel, you could be spending minutes or days on getting the same data on sales performance analyzed. However, being able to exploit the power of Excel would definitely help you to progress beyond your current level of work ability, efficiency and productivity.

If you are not sure if this is a course you should attend, simply download the excel file from the following web address http://www.synergyworks.com.sg/Excel_Test.html and find out if you could get the correct information asked for in 1 minute. If you are unable to, attending this course would then be extremely valuable for you.

Course Outline

The course is divided into 2 parts, lasting a total of 1½ days. The course is conducted with a class of no more than 18 participants.

PART ONE

The first part of the course is a full day session. During this day, 6 case scenarios will be used to share with participants our knowledge and experience in business intelligence, from turning raw data into useful business information to analyzing the business data for reporting and decision making. We will also share how to create macro with ZERO knowledge about programming.

PART TWO

The second part of the course is a half-day session, which is conducted one week after the first part. This lesson is customized based on the needs, skill level, expectation and requests of the participants.

251

Our Methods

Taking a hands-on approach and making use of common business decision making scenarios, participants will learn how to apply useful Excel functions and worksheet formulas to the process of sales performance, from data manipulation to sales performance reporting/analysis.

Part One Case Scenarios

CASE 1 | Translating Data

Translate Raw Data Into Useful Business Information

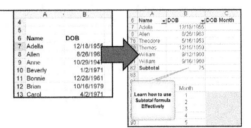

CASE 2 | Selecting Records

Select all records that meet a certain criteria (such as blank cells, contains conditional formats, visible rows, etc) at once using a simple and yet rarely explored function in Excel.

CASE 3 | Building Formulas

Build formulas that can intelligently and accurately:
> Retrieve the information from the database
> Merge records from two lists together
> Remove duplicates from the list, etc.

Our Methods

everyday Excel
Business Lab Pte Ltd

Taking a hands-on approach and making use of common business decision making scenarios, participants will learn how to apply useful Excel functions and worksheet formulas to the process of sales performance, from data manipulation to sales performance reporting/analysis.

Part One Case Scenarios

CASE 4 Analyzing Data

Analyze data contained within an Excel workbook using pivot table, a popular and powerful business intelligence tool provided by Microsoft Excel.

1. Summarize the data using pivot table
2. Create a new view with the mouse

CASE 5 Retrieving Databases

Learn how to retrieve office database records without having to do any export and import, and get up to date reports at regular intervals.

CASE 6 Automating Processes

Learn how to automate work processes even when having ZERO knowledge on Macro programming.

Apply all these worksheet functions and formulas in the case scenarios >>

1. Working with Date Functions
2. Working with Sub-Total Functions
3. Working with IF functions
4. Using Auto filters
5. Using GoTo
6. Counting records based on criteria
7. Getting relevant data from a cell
8. Merging data from two lists of records
9. Using Pivot Table
10. MS Query
11. Handle errors in formulas
12. Introduction to Macro Programming

253

everyday Excel

Business Lab Pte Ltd

A Revolutionary Approach
to *Excel Budgeting*

The Great Escape from Spreadsheet Hell

IN A SURVEY DONE FOR CORPORATE BUDGETING, IT WAS FOUND that 78% of all companies still use Excel as their primary budgeting and planning tool. And this is not limited to small and medium sized companies. 68% of large companies still use Excel as their primary budgeting and planning tool.

Most of these companies, however, experienced, Spreadsheet Hell, a term used to describe the following problems encountered as they developed and managed their budgeting template and model:

1. Fear of broken links when changing the cell locations of values in a worksheet.

2. Cumbersome to manage a group of workbooks that are inter-dependent on each other.

3. Laborious copying and pasting of data to and from a worksheet.

4. Unable to perform detailed analysis with the information stored in the worksheets and workbook.

5. No confidence that the information is accurately reflected in the workbooks.

6. Time taken to update workbooks becomes longer each time.

7. Too many cross links between workbooks.

8. Too many cross links between worksheets within each workbook.

9. How data in different worksheets are linked together is forgotten.

If you are being afflicted by this Spreadsheet Hell, attend this course whereby you will be trained on how to use our revolutionary solution to escape from *Spreadsheet Hell!*

✓ Course Outline

You will learn how to develop a business model using excel which can:

1. Create a Data Hub without links;

2. Analyze the budget in different dimensions such as distribution channels, product groups, divisions, countries, using the Data Hub;

3. Create powerful and professional looking reports and charts that are automatically updated with new budget items added into the Data Hub.

1

Align the headers and sub-headers with the data inputs

2

Transform the data inputs into a Data Cluster.

255

Course Outline

3 Analyze the business units' numbers using the Data Cluster

4 Combine all the Data Clusters into a Data Hub

✓ Course Outline

5 Analyze budget at business unit level

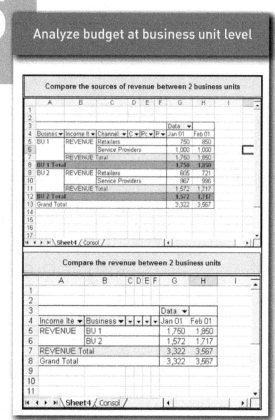

6 Prepare dashboard, summary reports and charts using the Data Hub

For Course Enquires Contact:

everydayExcel Business Lab Pte Ltd
15 West Coast Highway #02-07
Pasir Panjang Building
Singapore 117861
Tel : 65-6873 9946
Fax: 65-6795 7250

www.everydayexcel.com
Email: jason.khoo@synergyworks.com.sg

www.ingramcontent.com/pod-product-compliance
Lightning Source LLC
LaVergne TN
LVHW062311060326
832902LV00013B/2154